General Educational Development Testing Service
A Program of the American Council on Education®

Dear GED Candidate:

Congratulations on taking one of the most important steps of your life—earning a GED credential!

Since 1942, millions of people like you have taken the GED Tests to continue their education, to get a better job, or to achieve a sense of accomplishment.

We are delighted to introduce **Keys to GED® Success: Language Arts, Reading**—an invaluable resource to help you pass the GED Language Arts, Reading Test. It has been developed through a partnership between the GED Testing Service®–developer of the GED Tests–and Steck-Vaughn, a leading provider of GED test preparation materials and the exclusive distributor of the Official GED Practice Tests.

GEDTS researched the types of skills that GED candidates could focus on to improve their chances of passing the tests. We identified the types of questions and possible reasons that test-takers were missing specific questions on each test and decided to share that information. GEDTS collaborated with Steck-Vaughn to target those skills in a workbook that would benefit present and future GED candidates. The skills targeted in our research are called the **GED® Key Skills**—which is what you'll find in this book. In addition to the **GED Key Skills**, this book includes other important lessons that are needed to pass the GED Language Arts, Reading Test.

To help GED teachers, there is a Teaching Tips section included. The tips are written to address teaching strategies for some of the key problem areas that emerged from our research.

As the owner of this book, you can use the Pretest to determine exactly which skills you need to target to pass the test. Once you have completed your study, you can determine whether you are ready to take the GED Language Arts, Reading Test by taking an Official GED Practice Test—which follows Lesson 20. The GED Testing Service has developed this practice test as a predictor of the score that you will likely earn on the actual GED Language Arts, Reading Test.

Remember that there are four other books in the **Keys to GED Success** series. These other books cover the remaining four GED Tests: Language Arts, Writing, Science, Social Studies, and Mathematics. All titles in this series are available exclusively from Steck-Vaughn.

We wish you the best of luck on the GED Tests.

Sylvia E. Robinson
Executive Director
GED® Testing Service

September 2008

One Dupont Circle NW, Washington, DC 20036-1193
Telephone: 202/939.9490   Fax: 202/659.8875
www.acenet.edu   www.GEDtest.org

# *Keys to*
# GED® SUCCESS

## Language Arts, Reading

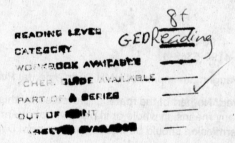

Steck
Vaughn™

HOUGHTON MIFFLIN HARCOURT
Supplemental Publishers

www.SteckVaughn.com/AdultEd
800-531-5015

ISBN-10: 1-4190-5349-3
ISBN-13: 978-1-4190-5349-8

© 2009 Steck-Vaughn, an imprint of HMH Supplemental Publishers Inc.

Steck-Vaughn is a trademark of HMH Supplemental Publishers Inc.

Official GED® Practice Language Arts, Reading Test Form PA © 2001, American Council on Education

Printed in the United States of America.

1 2 3 4 5 6 7 8 9 022 15 14 13 12 11 10 09 08

# [ Contents ]

KEY **This symbol indicates GED® Key Skills as identified by the GED Testing Service®**

*Keys to GED® Success: Language Arts, Reading* has been prepared by Steck-Vaughn in cooperation with the GED Testing Service®. This book focuses on the thinking skills needed to pass the GED Language Arts, Reading Test.

This book also identifies the *GED® Key Skills*, which are skills that the GED Testing Service® has pinpointed as those most often missed by test takers who come close to passing the GED Tests. For more information about these skills see *A Message from the GED Testing Service®* at the front of this book.

In this book, the *GED Key Skills* are identified by this symbol: **KEY**

It is recommended that students who are preparing to take the GED Tests follow this plan:

**1. Take the Language Arts, Reading Pretest.**
   While it is best to work through all the lessons in this book, students can choose to focus on specific skills. The *Language Arts, Reading Pretest* assesses the 20 skills in this book. The *Pretest Performance Analysis Chart* on page 9 will help students to target the skills that need the most attention.

**2. Work through the 4-page skill lessons in the book.**
   • The first page of each lesson provides an approach to the skill and to thinking through the questions. Students should carefully read the step-by-step thinking strategies and pay attention to the explanations of why the correct answers are right and why the wrong answer choices are incorrect.

   • The second page of each lesson contains sample GED questions. Students should use the hints and the answers and explanations sections to improve their understanding of how to answer questions about each skill.

   • The third and fourth pages of each lesson present GED practice questions that allow students to apply the skill to the same types of questions that they will see on the test.

Students should use the *Answers and Explanations* at the back of this book to check their answers and to learn more about how to make the correct answer choices.

**3. Take the *Official GED® Practice Test Form PA: Language Arts, Reading* in this book and analyze the results.**

The half-length practice test at the end of this book is the Official GED Practice Test Form PA–developed by the GED Testing Service®. Taking this test allows students to evaluate how well they will do on the actual GED Language Arts, Reading Test.

Based on the results, test administrators can determine if the student is ready to take the actual test. Those students who are not ready will need more study and should use the other GED Language Arts, Reading preparation materials available from Steck-Vaughn, which are listed at the back of this book and can be found at www.SteckVaughn.com/AdultEd.

**4. Prior to taking the GED Language Arts, Reading Test, take an additional Official GED Practice Test.**

The more experience that students have taking practice tests, the better they will do on the actual test. For additional test practice, they can take the Full-Length Practice Test Form or any of the other Official GED Practice Tests available from Steck-Vaughn at www.SteckVaughn.com/AdultEd.

By using this book and the others in this series, students will have the information and strategies developed by both the GED Testing Service® and experienced adult educators, so that they can reach their goal—passing the GED Tests.

# Teaching Tips

Below is an interactive teaching strategy that supports and develops a specific *GED*® *Key Skill*.

## Integrate Outside Information (Reading KEY Skill 20)

Discuss that one type of question on the GED Language Arts, Reading Test requires students to: 1) read some additional information that is provided as a part of the question and 2) combine it with information in the passage. These questions can present additional information about: events that happen earlier or later in the work, some biographical information about the author, or a selection from the review of the work.

- Students read the passages in Key Skill 20.
- In pairs, students carefully read the questions that accompany each passage and decide which questions provide additional information.
  - For those questions, they should identify the new information in the question stem by writing it on a sheet of paper.
  - The partners should discuss how to relate the new information to the passage:
    - *Does it give new information about the passage?*
    - *Does it give an additional insight into the passage or the author?*
    - *Does it help me understand the passage in a new way?*
  - The partners should select the correct answer choice and share their choices with the class.

## Language Arts, Reading Test Skill-Building Strategies

GED Testing Service® research determined that implementing the following suggestions can help to improve scores on the GED Language Arts, Reading Test.

**Students should read as much as possible outside of class.** Reading more frequently will help students pass all of the GED Tests, including the Language Arts, Reading Test. Students should challenge themselves with increasingly longer reading materials and more advanced vocabulary.

**Students should prepare to read a variety of texts.** Students should have experience reading fiction and non-fiction prose.

- Fiction includes excerpts from short stories, novels, poems, and plays.
  - Some of the fiction that appears on the test is from the genre of fantastical/imaginative fiction, including fantasy and science fiction. Since these types of passages seem especially challenging to students, discussion of this genre and exposure to readings from them will be beneficial to students.
- Non-fiction includes biography, autobiography, speeches, and essays as well as informational materials, such as community and workplace documents.
  - Teachers and students can bring in brochures, pamphlets, memos, and handbooks. Students can work in pairs and write questions for each other based on:
    - *Asking the other student to find specific information.*
    - *Asking the other student to describe the intended audience and the purpose of the piece.*
    - *Asking the other student to evaluate if there is enough clear information to utilize the piece in a specific situation. If not, students can identify what additional information would be needed.*

**In preparing for the test and during the test itself, students should read an entire excerpt before answering the questions based on it.** Questions can be based on introductory text (set off by square brackets at the beginning of excerpts), stage directions in drama excerpts, and text that is not specifically referenced by line numbers.

**When answering test questions, students should make sure that they are answering the questions based on the information in the passage.** In some cases, answer choices may be true statements, but they do not answer the specific question that is being asked.

# Language Arts, Reading Pretest

## Directions

This pretest consists of 20 questions designed to measure how well you know skills needed to pass the GED Language Arts, Reading Test. There is one question for each of the 20 lessons in this book.

- Take the pretest and record your answers on the *Pretest Answer Sheet* found on page 123. Choose the <u>one best answer</u> to each question.

- Check your answers in the *Pretest Answers and Explanations* section, which starts on page 103. Reading the explanations for the answers will help you understand why the correct answers are right and the incorrect answer choices are wrong.

- Fill in the *Pretest Performance Analysis Chart* on page 9 to determine which skills are the most important for you to focus on as you work in this book.

..................................................................................................................................................

<u>Questions 1 and 2</u> refer to the following poem.

## WHAT DOES THE SPEAKER VALUE?

### The Coin

Into my heart's treasury
I slipped a coin
That time cannot take
Nor a thief purloin—
(5) Oh better than the minting
Of a gold-crowned king
Is the safe-kept memory
Of a lovely thing.

Sara Teasdale

1. What is the "heart's treasury" in the poem?

   (1) the pleasure of physical health
   (2) an attitude toward time
   (3) the feeling of financial security
   (4) the things a person values
   (5) a sense of deep regret

2. What does the coin most likely symbolize in this poem?

   (1) memory of a lost love
   (2) a hard lesson learned
   (3) slow progress toward security
   (4) the growth of wisdom
   (5) memory of a special experience

Questions 3 through 5 refer to the following passage.

## WHAT CHANGES HAVE BEEN MADE TO THE POLICY?

Dear Member:

Enclosed is the Endorsement Rider for your CareMax Health Insurance Policy. Please review it and attach it to your policy.

The Rider details certain changes to your CareMax policy. These changes are required by recent bills passed by the Legislature. The changes to the policy are summarized below.

1. The Eligibility section is amended regarding persons who are ineligible for CareMax coverage. A person whose prior CareMax coverage was terminated for nonpayment of premium (lapse) cannot receive coverage for 18 months from the termination date.

2. The deductible provision in Section 7 of the policy is amended to allow a change to a higher deductible at any time during the calendar year. Only one change per calendar year is allowed, and that change must be an increase in deductible.

Please call your CareMax representative if you have any questions.

3. What is the best restatement of the second paragraph?

(1) Your policy is unaffected by the recent changes in Legislature.
(2) The Rider details certain changes to your CareMax policy.
(3) Only one change per calendar year is allowed.
(4) CareMax is a part of the Legislature.
(5) Because of recent Legislature decisions, CareMax had to make changes to their policies.

4. What is the best summary of the second change?

(1) You can now increase your deductible at any time during a year, but only once.
(2) You can now change your deductible once a year.
(3) You can now change to a lower deductible at any time.
(4) A person is ineligible for coverage for 18 months if termination of original coverage was due to nonpayment.
(5) You can now decrease your deductible once a year.

5. Which of these statements is an inference supported by the passage?

(1) Only one deductible change per calendar year is allowed.
(2) You can now change to a lower deductible at any time.
(3) The Legislature does not consider your best interests when passing laws.
(4) The Legislature can affect insurance coverage within the United States.
(5) A Rider is your CareMax representative.

Questions 6 through 8 refer to the following passage.

## WHAT SHOULD EMPLOYEES DO?

Memorandum
To: All SYD employees
From: Norma Chausovsky
Date: June 30, 2009
RE: Dry-erase Boards

I am glad that many of you are taking advantage of our new flexible work schedule. The new hours allow us to work from home or the office depending on company needs. I know it is important for you to be able to go to doctor's appointments, visit your children's schools, or just run errands during the day. In order to keep this new freedom, we must all work together to avoid problems.

The biggest problem noted so far is inter-office communication. Scheduling meetings has become very difficult, and employees have been wasting valuable work time and energy trying to track down their team members. In order to remedy this time problem, we will be installing a dry-erase board outside of each cubicle. Please write your regular office hours at the top of your board. Whenever you leave your cubicle, make a note at the bottom of the dry-erase board to indicate what time you will return. With your help, we will all enjoy flexible scheduling.

6. What is the main idea of the passage?
   (1) The company has a new flexible work schedule.
   (2) The flexible work schedule isn't working well.
   (3) Using dry-erase boards will help remedy the main problem of the flexible work schedule.
   (4) Dry-erase boards are being installed.
   (5) Scheduling meetings has become very difficult.

7. Employers believe flexible work schedules are popular because the increased flexibility allows employees to handle the competing demands of work and personal interests.

   Based on this information, which statement is probably true about the employees of SYD?

   (1) They cannot budget time.
   (2) They are able to balance home and work life more efficiently now.
   (3) They spend more time at work than at home.
   (4) They spend more time at home than at work.
   (5) They lead busier lives than most others.

8. What is an opinion from the passage?

   (1) Dry-erase boards are being installed outside of each cubicle.
   (2) We will all enjoy flexible scheduling.
   (3) Many employees are using the new flexible work schedule.
   (4) Employees have used the flexible hours to go to doctor's appointments.
   (5) The biggest problem noted so far is inter-office communication.

Questions 9 through 12 refer to the following excerpt from a novel.

## WHAT IS THE CONFLICT?

One A.M. Peter and July broke into the captain's cabin. The curtain was pulled across the berth, a heavy blue cambric which also covered the porthole, shutting out the sun when the captain wanted to sleep. Tentatively, Peter pulled back the curtain, possessed by the wild notion that Captain Regan was hiding in his bunk and would leap up and choke him. The berth was empty,

(5) of course. In the hanging locker he found what they were looking for—the wide-brimmed black hat, a pistol, and a smooth-bore gun. Peter threw the musket to July and shoved the pistol into his waistband. Then he picked up the hat. Suppose it didn't fit? Suppose it was too big and fell down over his eyes blinding him?

"What's so funny?" July asked, a frown on his handsome face at the absurdity of anything

(10) being funny on this menacing day.

"The captain's hat. She's a perfect fit."

"Naturally. You both fatheads."

Peter grinned. "Let's get on back—"

Brother Man interrupted him, sticking his big head through the door. "You better hurry up on

(15) deck, Peter. Turno's about to kill Aaron."

With an oath, Peter hurried topside. The burly fireman had cross-eyed Aaron backed up against the rail, choking him. The crew was hollering, "Let him go," but making no move to interfere except for Stretch.

"For God's sake, man," Stretch yelled, grabbing Turno's arm.

(20) The fireman snatched it free and socked him. The blow dropped Stretch to his knees. Turno lifted Aaron off his feet while squeezing his neck, the deckhand's eyes rolling around like loose pebbles in his head. "Loose him," Peter yelled running forward. He snatched the pistol from his waistband and reaching the fireman jabbed it into his side. "I ain't fooling, Turno. Let him go."

Turno released Aaron so suddenly that the man stumbled and fell. Kneeling on the ground and

(25) rubbing his neck he blubbered. "He were gon kill me, Peter."

The fireman stared at him with contempt. "You is a lie. I was gonna toss you overboard only half dead and let the sharks finish you off."

Louise Meriwether, *Fragments of the Ark*

9. What is the most likely plot and setting of the events represented in this excerpt?

  (1) growing up in a seacoast town
  (2) a conflict between soldiers in wartime
  (3) a mutiny on a ship
  (4) gang warfare in a city
  (5) not enough information is provided

10. Which of the following best describes the overall structure of this passage?

  (1) A playwright creates a drama through dialog.
  (2) A writer makes a main point and then uses details to support it.
  (3) A narrator describes fictional events occurring in time order.
  (4) A writer explains the causes and effects of an occurrence.
  (5) A poet describes the metaphorical struggle between good and evil.

11. How does the author reveal the various characters of Peter, July, Turno, and Aaron?

  (1) gives an analysis of the personality of each character
  (2) shows what each character is wearing
  (3) gives an inside look at what each character is thinking
  (4) uses their speeches to reveal their different personalities
  (5) describes the physical characteristics of each character

12. What implication about the overall situation is made by the events that occur between Aaron, Turno, and Peter?

  (1) These are rough people who may turn on each other.
  (2) Their efforts are almost certainly doomed to failure.
  (3) Aaron has brought misfortune upon them all.
  (4) July is the only one who is innocent in the whole matter.
  (5) They are on a course of action for a good and admirable cause.

Questions 13 through 16 refer to the following excerpt from a play.

# WHO LOVES WHOM?

**HERMIA:** God speed fair Helena! Whither away?

**HELENA:** Call you me fair? that fair again unsay.
Demetrius loves your fair: O happy fair!
Your eyes are lode-stars; and your tongue's sweet air
(5)     More tuneable than lark to shepherd's ear,
When wheat is green, when hawthorn buds appear.
Sickness is catching: O, were favour so,
Yours would I catch, fair Hermia, ere I go;
My ear should catch your voice, my eye your eye,
(10)   My tongue should catch your tongue's sweet melody.
Were the world mine, Demetrius being bated,
The rest I'd give to be to you translated.
O, teach me how you look, and with what art
You sway the motion of Demetrius' heart.

(15) **HERMIA:** I frown upon him, yet he loves me still.

**HELENA:** O that your frowns would teach my smiles such skill!

**HERMIA:** I give him curses, yet he gives me love.

**HELENA:** O that my prayers could such affection move!

**HERMIA:** The more I hate, the more he follows me.

(20) **HELENA:** The more I love, the more he hateth me.

**HERMIA:** His folly, Helena, is no fault of mine.

**HELENA:** None, but your beauty: would that fault were mine!

**HERMIA:** Take comfort: he no more shall see my face;
Lysander and myself will fly this place.
(25)   Before the time I did Lysander see,
Seem'd Athens as a paradise to me:
O, then, what graces in my love do dwell,
That he hath turn'd a heaven unto a hell!

William Shakespeare, *A Midsummer Night's Dream*

13. How are Helena and Hermia different?

   (1) Hermia loves both Lysander and
       Demetrius.
   (2) Demetrius loves Helena while Lysander
       loves Hermia.
   (3) Hermia loves Lysander while Helena
       loves Demetrius.
   (4) Helena loves Lysander while Hermia
       loves Demetrius.
   (5) Lysander loves Helena while Demetrius
       loves Hermia.

14. What effect does Hermia's hate in line 19
    have?

   (1) It makes Demetrius love her more.
   (2) It makes Lysander love her more.
   (3) It makes Demetrius hate her.
   (4) It makes Lysander hate her.
   (5) It makes Helena hate her.

15. What has been turned into hell for Hermia
    (line 28)?

   (1) her youth
   (2) her home
   (3) her best friend
   (4) her love
   (5) her good looks

16. If these characters lived in the 21st century,
    what medical procedure would Helena be
    most likely to have?

   (1) liposuction to be thinner
   (2) donating a kidney to save Hermia's life
   (3) LASIK to correct her bad vision
   (4) plastic surgery to look more like Hermia
   (5) teeth whitening to brighten her teeth
       and smile

Questions 17 through 20 refer to the following excerpt from a short story.

## WHAT IS THIS WOMAN FEELING?

I don't like our room a bit. I wanted one downstairs that opened on the piazza and had roses all over the windows, and such pretty old fashioned chintz hangings. But John would not hear of it.

(5) He said there was only one window and not room for two beds, and no near room for him if he took another.

He is very careful and loving, and hardly lets me stir without special direction.

I have a schedule prescription for each hour in the day; he takes all care from me, and so I feel basely ungrateful not to value it more.

He said that we came here solely on my account, that I was to have perfect rest and all the air I
(10) could get. "Your exercise depends on your strength, my dear," he said "and your food somewhat on your appetite; but air you can absorb all the time." So we took the nursery at the top of the house.

It is a big, airy room, the whole floor nearly, with windows that look all ways, and air and sunshine galore. It was nursery first and then playroom and gymnasium, I should judge; for the
(15) windows are barred for little children, and there are rings and things in the walls.

The paint and paper look as if a boys' school had used it. It is stripped off—the paper—in great patches all around the head of my bed, about as far as I can reach, and in a great place on the other side of the room low down. I never saw a worse paper in my life. One of those sprawling flamboyant patterns committing every artistic sin...
(20) The color is repellant, almost revolting; a smouldering unclean yellow, strangely faded by the slow-turning sunlight. It is a dull yet lurid orange in some places, a sickly silver tin in others.

No wonder the children hated it! I should hate it myself if I had to live in this room long.

There comes John, and I must put this away—he hates to have me write a word.

Charlotte Perkins Gillman, "The Yellow Wallpaper"

17. What conclusion can you draw from this excerpt about John?

(1) John prefers for others to be in control.
(2) John is a rich and experienced traveler.
(3) John's favorite color is yellow.
(4) John once ran a school for boys.
(5) John doesn't consider others' feelings.

18. What is the most likely theme of this story?

(1) Some people imprison others while trying to protect them.
(2) Travel is not always a pleasant experience.
(3) The physical environment has a lot to do with one's mood.
(4) Some buildings cannot easily be repurposed for other uses.
(5) Without physical health, little matters in life.

19. What does the narrator's comment about the "sprawling flamboyant patterns" (lines 18–19) suggest about the narrator?

(1) She is intolerant of others.
(2) She has unusual tastes.
(3) She has conservative tastes.
(4) She enjoys showy fashions.
(5) She prefers solid colors.

20. Which of the following expressions best represents the tone of the woman's narration?

(1) overwhelminghy angry
(2) joyously surprised
(3) wonderingly confused
(4) privately sad
(5) mysteriously secretive

# Pretest Performance Analysis Chart

The following chart can help you to determine your strengths and weaknesses on the skill areas needed to pass the official GED Language Arts, Reading Test.

- Use the *Pretest Answers and Explanations* on pages 103–105 to check your answers.
- On the chart below:
    - Circle the question numbers that you answered correctly.
    - Put a check mark (✓) next to the skills for which you answered the questions incorrectly.
    - Use the page numbers to find the lessons that you need to target as you work.

| Question Number | Skills to Target (✓) | GED Language Arts, Reading Skill Lessons | Page Numbers |
|---|---|---|---|
| 6 | | **Skill 1:** Identify the Main Idea | 10–13 |
| 3 | | **Skill 2:** Restate Information | 14–17 |
| 4 | | **Skill 3:** Summarize Ideas | 18–21 |
| 12 | | **Skill 4:** Identify Implications | 22–25 |
| 15 | | **Skill 5:** Get Meaning from Context | 26–29 |
| 16 | | **Skill 6:** Apply Ideas to a New Context | 30–33 |
| 5 | | **Skill 7:** Make Inferences | 34–37 |
| 14 | | **Skill 8:** Identify Causes and Effects | 38–41 |
| 8 | | **Skill 9:** Distinguish Fact and Opinion | 42–45 |
| 2 | | **Skill 10:** Interpret Symbols and Imagery | 46–49 |
| 1 | | **Skill 11:** Interpret Figurative Language | 50–53 |
| 11 | | **Skill 12:** Analyze Characterization | 54–57 |
| 9 | | **Skill 13:** Interpret Plot and Setting | 58–61 |
| 19 | | **Skill 14:** Analyze Word Choice | 62–65 |
| 17 | | **Skill 15:** Draw Conclusions | 66–69 |
| 10 | | **Skill 16:** Interpret Overall Style and Structure | 70–73 |
| 20 | | **Skill 17:** Interpret Tone of a Piece | 74–77 |
| 18 | | **Skill 18:** Determine Theme | 78–81 |
| 13 | | **Skill 19:** Compare and Contrast | 82–85 |
| 7 | | **Skill 20:** Integrate Outside Information | 86–89 |

# Skill 1

# Identify the Main Idea

A **main idea** is the most important point an author is trying to make in a paragraph or passage. The main idea is a statement that sums up the paragraph or passage. Other details and information provide support for the main idea. These details may be facts, information, or images that help to convey the main idea convincingly. Do not confuse a strong supporting detail with the main idea itself. Try to sum up the main idea in a sentence.

Sometimes a main idea is **explicit**, or directly stated in a single sentence. This clear statement of the main idea is often at the beginning or end of a passage. Sometimes the main idea is **implied**. The author hints at, or implies, the main idea through ideas or details in the passage.

**Read the passage. Choose the <u>one best answer</u> to the question.**

And besides, human society had done him nothing but harm; he had never seen anything of it save that angry face which it calls Justice, and which it shows to those whom it strikes. Men had only touched him to bruise him. Every contact with them had been a blow. Never, since his infancy, since the days of his mother, of his sister, had he ever encountered a friendly word and a kindly glance. From suffering to suffering, he had gradually arrived at the conviction that life is a war; and that in this war he was the conquered. He had no other weapon than his hate. He resolved to sharpen it in prison and to bear it away with him when he departed.

based on *Les Miserables* by Victor Hugo

**QUESTION:** Which of the following <u>best</u> expresses the main idea of this passage?

(1) The man has suffered many beatings through the years.
(2) The man was a soldier on the losing side of a war.
(3) The man has spent years in prison and will soon leave.
(4) The man feels injured by and bitter toward life.
(5) The man has felt kindness only from his mother and sister.

## EXPLANATIONS

**STEP 1**

To answer this question, ask yourself:
- What is the topic of this passage? What is it about? <u>how a man's life, filled with violence and suffering, has led to a feeling of defeat and hatred</u>
- What is the question asking me to do? <u>Choose the option that best sums up the main idea, or most important point, of the passage.</u>

**STEP 2**

Evaluate the answer choices. Which sentence <u>best</u> expresses the main idea?

(1) No. The "blows," which may be real or just an expression, are a reason for his bitterness, not the main idea of the passage.
(2) No. The "war" is not a real war; it is a metaphor about life.
(3) No. We do not know when he will leave prison, and his departure date is not the main idea.
(4) **Yes. Everything that has happened in his life has led him to feel angry and bitter.**
(5) No. The passage reveals very little about his mother and sister.

**ANSWER: (4) The man feels injured by and bitter toward life.**

# Practice the Skill

Try these examples. Choose the <u>one best answer</u> to each question. Then check your answers and read the explanations.

## WHICH TYPE OF EMPLOYER IS BEST?

Would you rather work in a small company or a large corporation? If the size of your employer is important to you, evaluate the advantages and disadvantages of both options.

Big businesses can afford to offer employees a substantial benefits package. Many workers today consider good health insurance to be an essential benefit. Large corporations

(5)  may also offer more flexible work arrangements such as telecommuting, staggered hours, or compressed work weeks.

Smaller companies, too, have their advantages. A primary one is the fact that small business employers often use layoffs as their last choice when they need to reduce costs. In addition, workers who want more variety in their responsibilities find that small

(10)  companies allow them to use more of their skills and to develop new ones.

Most of us would agree that no job is perfect. However, to find satisfying long-term employment, a careful analysis of all options is essential. The size of an employer's operation is an important consideration when you choose where to work.

1. Which of the following <u>best</u> states the main idea of the third paragraph (lines 7–10)?

   (1) Smaller companies are better places to work.
   (2) Small business employers appear to use layoffs as a last choice to reduce costs.
   (3) Smaller companies also have advantages.
   (4) Smaller companies have more disadvantages.
   (5) Workers want more variety in their responsibilities.

   **HINT** What is the subject of the third paragraph? Which sentence tells you what the writer wants to say in the paragraph?

2. Which of the following <u>best</u> states the main idea of the entire passage?

   (1) Most of us would agree that no job is perfect.
   (2) Large corporations are more likely to offer flexible work options.
   (3) A prospective employee should analyze everything about an employer.
   (4) Small and large companies offer different types of advantages.
   (5) Many workers today consider good health insurance an essential benefit.

   **HINT** The main idea may not be directly stated in one sentence. As you read, try to think of a statement that expresses the main idea.

## Answers and Explanations

**1. (3) Smaller companies also have advantages.**

Option (3) is correct. This sentence from the passage is a clear statement of the main idea.

Options (1) and (4) incorrectly make claims that are nowhere in the passage. Option (2) is not the main idea; it's a supporting detail. Option (5) is incorrect because it is only one part of a detail, and it is wrongly stated.

**2. (4) Small and large companies offer different types of advantages.**

Option (4) accurately sums up the writer's ideas about the different advantages of small and large companies.

Options (1) and (3) do not cover all the advantages and disadvantages discussed in the passage. Options (2) and (5) are incorrect because they are details that express only part of the main idea.

# Identify the Main Idea

**Directions: Choose the <u>one best answer</u> to each question.**

<u>Questions 1 and 2</u> refer to the following passage.

## HOW HAS THE BOY'S LIFE CHANGED?

No more wet grounds, no more dikes and sluices, no more of these grazing cattle—though they seemed, in their dull manner to wear a little
(5)    more respectful air now, and to face round, in order that they might stare as long as possible at the possessor of such great expectations— farewell monotonous acquaintance of my
(10)   childhood, henceforth I was for London and greatness—not for smith's work in general and you! I made my exultant way to the old battery, and lying down there to consider the question of
(15)   whether Miss Havisham intended me for Estella, fell asleep.

When I awoke, I was much surprised to find Joe sitting beside me, smoking his pipe. He greeted me with a cheerful
(20)   smile on my opening my eyes and said:

"As being the last time, Pip, I thought I'd foller."

"And Joe, I am very glad you did so."

"Thankee, Pip."

(25)   "You may be sure, dear Joe," I went on, after we had shaken hands, "that I shall never forget you."

"No, no, Pip!" said Joe in a comfortable tone, "I'm sure of that. Aye, aye, old chap.
(30)   Bless you, it were only necessary to get it well round in a man's mind to be certain on it. But it took a bit of time to get it well round, the change come on so uncommon plump; didn't it?"

(35)   Somehow, I was not pleased with Joe's being so mightily secure of me. I should have liked him to have betrayed emotion, or to have said, "It does you credit Pip," or something of that sort.
(40)   Therefore I made no reply on his first head, merely saying as to his second that the tidings had indeed come suddenly, but that I had always wanted to be a gentleman, and had often and
(45)   often speculated on what I would do if I were one.

"Have you though?" said Joe. "Astonishing!"

Charles Dickens, *Great Expectations*

1. Which sentence <u>best</u> sums up the main idea of the passage?

   (1)  A youth who hates cattle is leaving the country to get married.
   (2)  A youth leaving home for the city is surprised that his friend accepts it.
   (3)  A youth leaving the city cannot get away from an old friend he dislikes.
   (4)  A youth leaving his home must deal with the grief of those he leaves behind.
   (5)  A youth who will soon be rich expects that others will want to share in his fortune.

2. What is the main idea of paragraph 7 (lines 28–34)?

   (1)  Joe is surprised at how long it's taken for Pip to leave.
   (2)  Joe doesn't think Pip will remember him.
   (3)  Joe is confident in his relationship with Pip.
   (4)  Joe doesn't really understand what has happened.
   (5)  Joe wishes Pip had made a different decision.

> **TIP**
>
> To find a main idea, look for a single sentence that applies to all details about the topic. If you cannot find one sentence that covers them all, ask yourself what single statement the details in the passage would support.

Questions 3 through 6 refer to the following passage.

## WHAT IS IT LIKE TO BE A DOG?

I happen to know a big black hunting poodle named Beau. Beau loves to go for walks in the woods, and at such times as I visit his owners this task of seeing Beau safely through his morning adventures is happily turned over to me.

Beau has eyes, of course, and I do not doubt that he uses them when he greets his human friends by proffering a little gift such as his food dish. After this formality, which dates to his puppyhood, is completed, Beau immediately reverts to the world of snuffles. As a long-time trusted friend, I have frequently tried to get Beau to thrust his head out of the world of smells and actually to see the universe. I have led him before the mirror in my bedroom and tried to persuade him to see himself, his own visible identity. The results, it turns out, are totally unsatisfactory if not ludicrous. Beau peers out from his black ringlets as suspiciously as an ape hiding in a bush. He drops his head immediately and pretends to examine the floor. It is evident that he detests this apparition, and has no intention of being cajoled into some dangerous and undoggy wisdom by my voice.

He promptly brings his collar and makes appropriate throaty conversation. To appease his wounded feelings, I set out for a walk in the woods. It is necessary to do this with a long chain and a very tight grasp upon it. Beau is a big, powerful animal, and ringlets or no he has come from an active and carnivorous past. Once in the woods all this past suddenly emerges. One is dragged willy-nilly through leaf, thorn, and thicket on intangible trails that Beau's swinging muzzle senses upon the wind.

Loren Eiseley, *The Invisible Pyram*

3. Which sentence best sums up the main idea of this passage?

   (1) Dogs and humans live in different worlds.
   (2) Dogs do not perceive as much as humans.
   (3) Humans live in a world of sight.
   (4) The narrator loves dogs.
   (5) Dogs fear their own reflections.

4. Which of the following details supports the main idea of the passage?

   (1) Beau uses his eyes to greet his human friends.
   (2) Beau loves to go for walks in the woods.
   (3) The narrator loves the smell of the woods.
   (4) The narrator frequently tries to get Beau to use his eyes more.
   (5) Beau is afraid of apes hiding in the bushes.

5. This passage provides an example of

   (1) a main idea expressed in a single sentence in the passage
   (2) an expression of emotion rather than ideas
   (3) a main idea implied by details and examples
   (4) a writer presenting scientific facts
   (5) a persuasive piece intended to change readers' minds about dogs

6. Based on the passage, what is most likely the intended purpose of this essay?

   (1) to make readers think more carefully about their choices of pets
   (2) to make readers think about what different living beings experience
   (3) to express admiration for the mind of his friend and companion, Beau
   (4) to explain the overall superiority of the human mind compared to that of a dog
   (5) to explore the nature of the ancient relationship between humans and dogs

**Answers and explanations start on page 107.**

# Restate Information

Questions on the GED Test may ask you to restate information or to recognize information restated from a passage. When you **restate** something, you express the same idea in different words. Restating information is a good way to make sure you understand it. You absorb the meaning and then express it in another way. In order to restate ideas or information effectively, you must understand the important parts of the information. Use your skills in identifying the main idea to help you. Pick out the important part of the message, and express it in a clear way that makes sense.

**Read the passage. Choose the <u>one best answer</u> to the question.**

> Into my heart an air that kills
> From yon far country blows:
> What are those blue remembered hills,
> What spires, what farms are those?
>
> That is the land of lost content,
> I see it shining plain,
> The happy highways where I went
> And cannot come again.

A. E. Housman, "A Shropshire Lad, XL"

**QUESTION:** Which of the following <u>best</u> restates the main idea of this poem?

(1) I am lost in a strange, blue farmland.
(2) This place seems familiar to me, but I cannot tell exactly why.
(3) In my youth I was happy, but I cannot return to the past.
(4) Air travel is more complicated now than it once was.
(5) Pollution has severely damaged the atmosphere of this region.

**EXPLANATIONS**

**STEP 1** To answer this question, ask yourself:
- What is the central idea of this passage? <u>The poet expresses sadness for lost youth.</u>
- What is the question asking me to do? <u>Express the main idea using different words.</u>

**STEP 2** Evaluate the answer choices. Which sentence <u>best</u> restates the main idea?

(1) No. The poet makes no mention of being lost.
(2) No. There is no confusion in the narrator's mind about what he recalls.
(3) **Yes. The poet sees the past as a happier, more carefree time never to be relived.**
(4) No. Air travel is not mentioned in the poem.
(5) No. The second stanza shows that the poem is not about the physical environment.

**ANSWER: (3) In my youth I was happy, but I cannot return to the past.**

# Practice the Skill

Try these examples. Choose the <u>one best answer</u> to each question. Then check your answers and read the explanations.

## WHAT IS THIS SCHOOLBOY FEELING?

Or if Mangan's sister came out on the doorstep to call her brother in to his tea we watched her from our shadow peer up and down the street. We waited to see whether she would remain or go in and, if she remained, we left our shadow and walked up to Mangan's steps resignedly. She was waiting for us, her figure defined by the light from the half-opened door. Her brother always teased her before he obeyed and I stood by the railings looking at her. Her dress swung as she moved her body and the soft rope of her hair tossed from side to side.

Every morning I lay on the floor in the front parlour watching her door. The blind was pulled down to within an inch of the sash so that I could not be seen. When she came out on the doorstep my heart leaped. I ran to the hall, seized my books, and followed her. I kept her brown figure always in my eye and, when we came near the point at which our ways diverged, I quickened my pace and passed her. This happened morning after morning. I had never spoken to her, except for a few casual words, and yet her name was like a summons to all my foolish blood.

James Joyce, "Araby"

**1.** What is this passage about?

(1) The narrator thought his friend's older sister was foolish.

(2) The narrator and his friend tried hard to stay out late in the evening.

(3) The narrator grew to increasingly dislike his friend's sister.

(4) The narrator liked to tease his friend's older sister.

(5) The narrator developed a crush on his friend's older sister.

> **HINT**  What happens in this passage? How do you know?

**2.** Which of the following is the <u>best</u> restatement of the last sentence of the passage?

(1) The narrator did not want to speak to his friend's sister.

(2) The narrator was too shy to talk to the girl, despite his feelings.

(3) The narrator was moved when the older sister called to him.

(4) The narrator tried to make conversation with his friend's sister.

(5) The narrator often called out the name of his friend's older sister.

> **HINT**  How does the school boy feel about Mangan's sister? Why might he not have spoken to her?

## Answers and Explanations

**1. (5) The narrator developed a crush on his friend's older sister.**
Option (5) is correct. The narrator is fascinated by his friend's sister, whom he observes every day.

Options (1) and (3) are incorrect because they do not restate information included in the passage. Option (2) is not correct because the point of the passage is the narrator's growing feelings, not the boys' desire to stay out late. Option (4) is incorrect because it is the brother who teases her, not the narrator.

**2. (2) The narrator was too shy to talk to the girl, despite his feelings.**
Option (2) correctly describes the narrator's shyness and powerful emotions.

Option (1) is incorrect because the passage does not state whether the narrator would like to talk to the girl. Option (3) is incorrect because the sister never speaks to him. Option (4) is incorrect because he does not try to talk to her. Option (5) is incorrect because the passage does not say he called her name.

# Restate Information

**Directions: Choose the one best answer to each question.**

Questions 1 through 3 refer to the following passage.

## WHAT MUST THE CONTRACTOR DO?

This Agreement is made effective on September 27, 2008, between Rocky Rhodes (the "Builder") with offices at 1622 Saguaro Circle, El Paso, TX 79901
(5) and Jane McClean (the "Contractor") of 2010 Sandia Street, El Paso, TX 79903 for the following described services.

1. ASSIGNMENT. The Contractor agrees to perform to the satisfaction
(10) of the Builder the following services on the terms and conditions contained herein, according to guidelines and specifications provided by the Builder, and as otherwise directed by the Builder:
(15) Provide pest control services for all residences in the Riata Ranch subdivision owned by the Builder, whether under construction or completed.

2. SCHEDULE. The Contractor shall
(20) provide the services as defined in Attachment A on the following schedule: Spray each house once a month on the first Monday of the month.

3. PAYMENT. In consideration of the
(25) Contractor's satisfactory performance of the assignment, the Builder agrees to pay the Contractor according to the Rate and Maximum Fee indicated below, based upon satisfactory performance by
(30) the Contractor and subject to the terms of this Agreement.
Rate: $0.33 per square foot treated
Maximum Fee: $500 per house
per month
(35) All payments will be made in accordance with Attachment B of this Agreement. Payments will be due upon performance of the service and after receipt by the Builder of an invoice rendered by the
(40) Contractor after approval of the service by the Builder.

1. Which sentence best restates the information in lines 1–7?

(1) Rocky Rhodes, Builder, and Jane McClean, Contractor, enter into an agreement starting September 27, 2008.
(2) Rocky Rhodes, Contractor, and Jane McClean, Builder, enter into an agreement on September 27, 2008.
(3) Both the Builder and the Contractor reside in El Paso, Texas.
(4) The Agreement is in effect until September 27, 2008.
(5) The Agreement is a binding contract.

2. Which sentence best restates the Contractor's assignment?

(1) The Contractor must satisfy the Builder's expectations for services.
(2) The Builder will direct the Contractor's work when the Agreement begins.
(3) The Contractor will supply pest control for residences in Riata Ranch subdivision.
(4) The Builder will complete construction on residences in the Riata Ranch subdivision.
(5) The Contractor will submit an invoice upon completion of her work.

3. Which of the following best restates the payment rate?

(1) thirty-three cents per square foot per residence
(2) five hundred dollars per residence plus thirty-three cents per square foot
(3) thirty-three cents per square foot or five hundred dollars, whichever is more
(4) thirty-three cents per square foot or five hundred dollars, whichever is less
(5) five hundred dollars per residence

Questions 4 through 7 refer to the following poem.

## WHAT IS THE WRITER'S MOOD?

### Dover Beach

The sea is calm tonight.
The tide is full, the moon lies fair
Upon the straits—on the French coast the light
(5) Gleams and is gone; the cliffs of England stand
Glimmering and vast, out in the tranquil bay.
Come to the window, sweet is the
(10) night air!
Only, from the long line of spray
Where the sea meets the moon–
blanched land, Listen! You hear the grating roar
(15) Of pebbles which the waves draw back, and fling,
At their return, up the high strand,
Begin, and cease, and then again begin,
With tremulous cadence slow, and bring
(20) The eternal note of sadness in.

Sophocles long ago
Heard it on the Aegean, and it brought
Into his mind the turbid ebb and flow
Of human misery; we
(25) Find also in the sound a thought,
Hearing it by this distant northern sea.

The Sea of Faith
Was once, too, at the full, and round earth's shore
(30) Lay like the folds of a bright girdle furled.
But now I only hear
Its melancholy, long, withdrawing roar,
Retreating, to the breath
Of the night wind, down the vast
(35) edges drear
And naked shingles of the world.

Ah, love, let us be true
To one another! for the world, which seems
To lie before us like a land of dreams,
(40) So various, so beautiful, so new,
Hath really neither joy, nor love, nor light,
Nor certitude, nor peace, nor help for pain;
And we are here as on a darkling plain
Swept with confused alarms of struggle
(45) and flight,
Where ignorant armies clash by night.

Matthew Arnold

4. Which sentence best restates the mood of lines 1–20?

(1) The beautiful evening brings peace.
(2) Storm clouds are gathering soon.
(3) It is a pleasant evening, but I feel sad.
(4) The crashing of the waves worries me.
(5) I wish you could join me here tonight.

5. Which sentence best restates the ideas of lines 21–26?

(1) The past has disappeared completely.
(2) We are not as our ancestors were.
(3) Life is better now than it was thousands of years ago.
(4) Ancient peoples saw life differently.
(5) People thousands of years ago felt as we feel.

6. The best restatement of Arnold's advice in lines 37–38 would be that

(1) love can conquer all
(2) we should take care of each other
(3) we must put aside our anger
(4) there is much to hope for
(5) we should struggle onward

7. Which sentence is the best restatement of the poet's ideas?

(1) Human minds are not affected by the forces of nature.
(2) The sea endures forever no matter what people do.
(3) Only in learning can we find true peace of mind.
(4) Love is all we can be sure of in an uncertain world.
(5) War is always a result of ignorance.

**TIP**

In long or difficult passages, try to restate the ideas of one small section or "chunk" at a time. Pay special attention to the beginnings and endings of passages.

**Answers and explanations start on page 107.**

# Skill 3

# Summarize Ideas

A **summary** is a brief description of a larger amount of information. You probably summarize information regularly without even realizing it. When you tell a friend about something you saw, you tell the main points of what happened; you don't tell every last detail.

To summarize something, determine what the main ideas are and how they are supported. Then briefly describe the ideas. A summary should not include many details, inferences, or opinions.

**Read the passage. Choose the <u>one best answer</u> to the question.**

The side of the ship made an opaque belt of shadow on the darkling glassy shimmer of the sea. But I saw at once something elongated and pale floating very close to the ladder. Before I could form a guess a faint flash of phosphorescent light, which seemed to issue suddenly from the naked body of a man, flickered in the sleeping water with the elusive, silent play of summer lightning in a night sky. With a gasp I saw revealed to my stare a pair of feet, the long legs, a broad livid back immersed right up to the neck in a greenish cadaverous glow. One hand, awash, clutched the bottom rung of the ladder.

Joseph Conrad, *The Secret Sharer*

QUESTION: Which of the following <u>best</u> summarizes this passage?

(1) A pale, floating form threatens a ship.
(2) The narrator sees what appears to be the glowing body of a man clutching the ladder on the side of the ship.
(3) Bathed in a light like lightning, the body of a man was hanging onto the bottom rung of the ladder on the narrator's ship.
(4) The narrator stares at the lifeless body of a man.
(5) In the midst of a storm, the narrator sees a man swimming in the sea.

EXPLANATIONS

**STEP 1**

To answer this question, ask yourself:
• What is this passage about? <u>The narrator is looking at the shadow the ship makes on the sea's surface. Suddenly, he sees something floating near the ship's ladder. It is the glowing body of a man floating in the water. The body's hand grips the ladder.</u>
• What is the question asking me to do? <u>Identify the best summary of the passage.</u>

**STEP 2**

Evaluate the answer choices. Which sentence is the <u>best</u> summary?

(1) No. This choice does not address the passage's main points and incorrectly implies that the form is threatening the ship.
(2) **Yes. This choice provides a brief, accurate description of the main points of the passage.**
(3) No. This includes details that are unneeded in a summary.
(4) No. This choice is too brief and does not include the main points.
(5) No. This choice inaccurately summarizes the passage, which makes no mention of a storm or that the man was swimming.

ANSWER: **(2) The narrator sees what appears to be the glowing body of a man clutching the ladder on the side of the ship.**

# Practice the Skill

## WHAT IS HIS VISION OF AMERICA?

O, let America be America again—
The land that never has been yet—
And yet must be—
The land where *every* man is free.
(5) The land that's mine—
The poor man's, Indian's, Negro's, ME—
Who made America,
Whose sweat and blood, whose faith and pain,
(10) Whose hand at the foundry, whose plow in the rain,
Must bring back our might dream again.
Sure, call me any ugly name you choose—
The steel of freedom does not stain.
(15) From those who live like leeches on the people's lives,
We must take back our land again,
America!

Langston Hughes, "Let America Be America Again"

1. Which statement <u>best</u> summarizes the first four lines of the poem?

(1) America was never a great country.
(2) We must recapture our former greatness.
(3) We have always been the land of opportunity.
(4) This nation is only a dream.
(5) America must realize its ideal of freedom for all.

**HINT** Review the start of the poem. What is the main point of those lines?

2. Which is the <u>best</u> summary of lines 13–18?

(1) Slurs will not keep the common people from fighting for equality.
(2) Name-calling is a steel sword that divides our country.
(3) Americans must fight any foreign power that threatens the land.
(4) Rich Americans must stop stealing from the poor.
(5) Freedom has always been purchased by hard labor.

**HINT** Which choice focuses on the main idea?

## Answers and Explanations

**1. (5) America must realize its ideal of freedom for all.**
Option (5) correctly summarizes the meaning and feeling of the first four lines, which look to the future of what America can be.

The lines don't discuss America's greatness (options 1 and 2), opportunity (option 3), or that America is only a dream (option 4).

**2. (1) Slurs will not keep the common people from fighting for equality.**
Option (1) correctly restates the message of lines 13–18.

Option (2) incorrectly connects "steel" with name-calling rather than "freedom." The poem does not mention foreign powers, rich Americans, or hard labor, so options (3), (4), and (5) are not correct.

# Summarize Ideas

**Directions: Choose the one best answer to each question.**

Questions 1 through 3 refer to the following passage.

## HOW SHOULD YOU CONNECT THIS APPLIANCE?

For the personal safety of the consumer, this appliance must be grounded. The appliance is furnished with a power supply cord with a
(5)  three-prong grounding plug. To minimize possible shock hazard, the cord on this appliance must be plugged into a matching three-prong, fully grounded wall receptacle.
(10)  Do not alter or modify the prongs on the power supply cord. Do not, under any circumstances, remove the power supply cord ground prong. Do not use the power supply cord with adapters or
(15)  extension cords. If the three-prong plug does not fit the desired outlet, you must have an appropriate outlet installed by a qualified electrician.

The receptacle should provide 115 volts,
(20)  60Hz, AC only, and be 15- or 20-ampere fused and properly grounded. Grounding must be in accordance with the National Electrical Code and all local codes.

It is the personal responsibility and
(25)  obligation of the consumer to install and use this product with a properly matching wall receptacle, or to have a receptacle installed by a qualified electrician. Failure to observe these
(30)  instructions could result in severe injury or death from electrical shock.

1. Which of the following is the best summary of the first paragraph (lines 1–9)?

   (1) The appliance only works when grounded.
   (2) Plugging the appliance into a grounded wall receptacle fully eliminates the possibility of getting a shock.
   (3) The appliance should be plugged into a three-prong, fully grounded receptacle.
   (4) The appliance must be plugged into the wall receptacle furnished.
   (5) The appliance comes plugged into a grounded receptacle.

2. Which of the following is the best summary of the second paragraph (lines 10–18)?

   (1) You must use the supplied power cord as the manufacturer intended.
   (2) You must contact an electrician to be sure the connection is safe.
   (3) You can change the connector only under certain circumstances.
   (4) A qualified electrician can install a properly grounded outlet.
   (5) The receptacle must provide 115 volts to the appliance.

3. Which of the following is the best summary of the third paragraph (lines 19–23)?

   (1) The receptacle's specifications are as follows: 115 volts, 60Hz, AC only, 15- or 20-ampere fused, fully grounded.
   (2) The receptacle must comply with the National Electrical Code.
   (3) The National Electrical Code tells how to ground receptacles.
   (4) Only grounded receptacles are in accordance with the National Electrical Code.
   (5) The receptacle must provide 115 volts and be properly grounded.

Questions 4 through 6 refer to the following passage.

## WHAT MUST SHE DO TO CHANGE HER SITUATION?

Next day new steps were to be taken; my plans could no longer be confined to my own breast; I must impart them in order to achieve their success. Having
(5) sought and obtained an audience of the superintendent during the noontide recreation, I told her I had a prospect of getting a new situation where the salary would be double what I now received (for
(10) at Lowood I only got fifteen pounds per annum), and requested she would break the matter for me to Mr. Brocklehurst, or some of the committee, and ascertain whether they would permit me to
(15) mention them as references. She obligingly consented to act as mediatrix in the matter. The next day she laid the affair before Mr. Brocklehurst, who said that Mrs. Reed must be written to, as
(20) she was my natural guardian. A note was accordingly addressed to that lady, who returned for answer, that 'I might do as I pleased: she had long relinquished all interference in my affairs.' This note
(25) went the round of the committee, and, at last, after what appeared to me most tedious delay, formal leave was given me to better my condition if I could; and an assurance added that, as I had always
(30) conducted myself well, both as teacher and pupil, at Lowood, a testimonial of character and capacity, signed by the inspectors of that institution, should forthwith be furnished me.

Charlotte Brontë, *Jane Eyre*

> **TIP**
>
> As you judge choices in a question about summarizing, look carefully at details in the summaries. Do they agree with the passage? Incorrect choices may include details that do not match information in the passage.

4. Which of the following best summarizes the steps that the narrator goes through?

   (1) The narrator secretly gets a new job, speaks to the superintendent, and gets permission to leave.
   (2) The superintendent summons the narrator, speaks to the committee, and provides a testimonial.
   (3) The superintendent offers a new job to the narrator, and the committee approves the job.
   (4) The narrator gets the superintendent's help, seeks approval from Mrs. Reed, and receives permission to get a new situation.
   (5) Mr. Brocklehurst contacts Mrs. Reed, gives the narrator a new job, and writes a letter to the inspectors.

5. Which of the following best summarizes the situation in the passage?

   (1) The narrator is changing jobs.
   (2) The narrator is being kicked out of Lowood.
   (3) Mr. Brocklehurst has found a new job for the narrator.
   (4) Mrs. Reed desires that the narrator move to a new location.
   (5) The superintendent is pleased with the narrator's performance.

6. Which of the following is the best summary of Mrs. Reed's reply (lines 22–24)?

   (1) Mrs. Reed is pleased to interfere.
   (2) Mrs. Reed does not want to be involved with the narrator.
   (3) Mrs. Reed does not give the narrator permission to move.
   (4) Mrs. Reed confirms that she is the narrator's guardian.
   (5) Mrs. Reed denies she ever knew the narrator.

**Answers and explanations start on page 108.**

# Skill 4

# Identify Implications

An **implication** is information that is hinted at but not stated directly. To identify implications, look closely at the meanings and shades of meaning of the words the author chooses. Evaluate information that is stated directly and consider the situation or circumstance. You can also use what you know of the world to identify implications. An implication may be as powerful as an idea that is expressed directly.

**Read the passage. Choose the <u>one best answer</u> to the question.**

"They have none of them much to recommend them," replied he; "they are all silly and ignorant like other girls; but Lizzy has something more of quickness than her sisters."

"Mr. Bennet, how can you abuse your own children in such a way? You take delight in vexing me. You have no compassion for my poor nerves."

"You mistake me, my dear. I have a high respect for your nerves. They are my old friends. I have heard you mention them with consideration these twenty years at least."

"Ah! You do not know what I suffer."

"But I hope you will get over it, and live to see many young men of four thousand a year come into the neighbourhood."

"It will be of no use to us, if twenty such should come since you will not visit them."

"Depend upon it, my dear, that when there are twenty, I will visit them all."

Jane Austen, *Pride and Prejudice*

**QUESTION:** What does this passage imply about Mr. and Mrs. Bennet's relationship?

(1) They have not been married for very long.
(2) They no longer have any affection for each other.
(3) Mr. Bennet thinks his wife's worries are silly.
(4) She loves their daughters and he does not.
(5) They are frequently angry at each other.

## EXPLANATIONS

**STEP 1**  To answer this question, ask yourself:
- What is this passage about? <u>Mr. Bennet teases Mrs. Bennet about her nerves and anxieties about new neighbors.</u>
- What is the question asking me to do? <u>Figure out what this implies about their relationship.</u>

**STEP 2**  Evaluate the answer choices. Which sentence <u>best</u> expresses the implied situation?

(1) No. Mr. Bennet teases that her nerves have been his "friends" for "twenty years at least."
(2) No. He teases her gently, which implies that he still cares about her.
(3) **Yes. Mr. Bennet's teasing and mildly mocking tone suggest that he does not take her concerns seriously.**
(4) No. Mr. Bennet's preference for Lizzy does not necessarily mean he doesn't love the others.
(5) No. There is no information that suggests how often they are angry.

**ANSWER: (3) Mr. Bennet thinks his wife's worries are silly.**

## HAS MISS KENTON CHANGED?

For the first twenty or so minutes, I would say we exchanged the sort of remarks strangers might; she inquired politely about my journey thus far, how I was enjoying my holiday, which towns and landmarks I had visited and so on. As we continued to talk, I must say I thought I began to notice further, more subtle changes which the years had wrought on her. For
(5)   instance, Miss Kenton appeared, somehow, slower. It is possible this was simply the calmness that comes with age, and I did try hard for some time to see it as such. But I could not escape the feeling that what I was really seeing was a weariness with life; the spark which had once made her such a lively, and at times volatile person seemed now to have gone. In fact, every now and then, when she was not speaking, when her face was in repose, I thought I glimpsed
(10)  something like sadness in her expression. But then again, I may well have been mistaken about this.

Kazuo Ishiguro, *The Remains of the Day*

1. What does the passage imply about Miss Kenton's life since she last saw the narrator?

   (1)  She has been happy.
   (2)  She has worked hard.
   (3)  She has traveled a great deal.
   (4)  She has been ill.
   (5)  She has been sad.

   **HINT**   What facts are stated about Miss Kenton's life? What things can you tell for certain? What things are implied?

2. What does the passage imply about the narrator's view of Miss Kenton?

   (1)  He knew her only slightly in the past.
   (2)  He doesn't care if she's changed.
   (3)  He doesn't want to admit she's changed.
   (4)  He has never been fond of Miss Kenton.
   (5)  He shares her view of life.

   **HINT**   How does the narrator seem to feel about Miss Kenton? How can you tell?

## Answers and Explanations

**1. (5)  She has been sad.**
Option (5) is the best choice because the passage implies that Miss Kenton may have experienced things since the narrator last saw her that may have brought a "weariness with life." In lines 9 and 10, the narrator says he "glimpsed something like sadness" in her face.

Option (1) is not correct because she shows no sign of happiness. Options (2), (3), and (4) are incorrect because there is nothing in the passage that implies her work life, travel, or illness.

**2. (3)  He doesn't want to admit she's changed.**
Option (3) is the best choice. Twice in the passage (lines 5–6 and 10–11) the narrator tries to find another explanation for the changes he thinks he sees in Miss Kenton.

Option (1) is incorrect; the narrator's observations imply he knew her well. Option (2) is not correct; the narrator implies a hope that she has not changed. Option (4) is not correct; nothing in the passage implies dislike for Miss Kenton. Option (5) is not correct; nothing suggests the two share a view of life.

# Identify Implications

<u>**Directions:**</u> **Choose the <u>one best answer</u> to each question.**

<u>Questions 1 through 5</u> refer to the following poem.

## CAN THE HEAVENS BE MEASURED?

### When I Heard the Learn'd Astronomer

When I heard the learn'd astronomer;
When the proofs, the figures, were ranged
   in columns before me;
When I was shown the charts and diagrams,
   to add, divide, and measure them;
When I, sitting, heard the astronomer,
   where he lectured with much applause in
   the lecture room,
How soon, unaccountable, I became tired
   and sick;
Till rising and gliding out I wander'd off by
   myself,
In the mystical moist night-air, and from time
   to time,
Look'd up in perfect silence at the stars.

                              Walt Whitman

1. The term "learn'd astronomer" as used in this poem implies

   (1) great wisdom
   (2) religious tradition
   (3) literary expertise
   (4) scientific knowledge
   (5) native folklore

2. What do the repetitions of the clauses beginning with "When" imply about the poet's experience at the lecture?

   (1) He finds the lecture boring and repetitious.
   (2) The lecturer has a lot of knowledge.
   (3) The subject of astronomy is vast.
   (4) The lecture was fast-paced and interesting.
   (5) The subject matter is well organized.

3. What does the poem imply about scientific knowledge?

   (1) It is the best tool we have for understanding nature.
   (2) It is of no value compared to poetry.
   (3) It can bring fame to those who master it.
   (4) It cannot explain everything.
   (5) It can be entertaining if well presented.

4. What does the poem imply about human knowledge of nature?

   (1) Most of it is incorrect.
   (2) It is more interesting than nature itself.
   (3) It is inadequate.
   (4) It needs to be well structured to be understood.
   (5) No one is interested in it.

5. What does the "perfect silence" with which the poet looks up imply about the universe?

   (1) The "learn'd astronomer" has said all that can be said.
   (2) Illness interferes with full appreciation of nature.
   (3) Human nature is as important as the physical universe.
   (4) Words are too limited to describe or measure it.
   (5) The stars are only one part of the mystery of space.

> **TIP**
>
> Implications can be revealed by actions. What is the circumstance? What do people do in the situation? What do they say or not say about what they experience?

## WILL THE TOWN BE READY?

This year, we need to begin sand-baggaing as soon as a hurricane is reported. If we start early, we should be able to protect our seafront property and

(5) still have plenty of time for individuals to stormproof their homes and businesses. If you are able to carry and stack sand-bags, please report to our sandbag captain, Barbara Muller, at the docks. If

(10) you are not able to lift sandbags, please contact James Nguyen to help in filling sandbags and providing food and coffee to workers.

Our community has grown over the past

(15) year, and we will need more emergency supplies than ever before. The following items are in short supply: blankets, medicine, clothing, and batteries. Having sufficient supplies on hand will allow

(20) the town of Sea Breeze to respond to any emergency quickly and to not have to depend on outside help this year.

The town council has printed hurricane awareness packets and distributed them

(25) to new residents. However, we would like volunteers to distribute the new packets to all residents and answer questions about emergency procedures. If you are willing to knock on doors, please contact

(30) Kelly Sorrentino at 256-8897.

We will also be setting up an information center at Town Hall. There will be a phone bank, and we need volunteers to answer phones and answer

(35) questions. Information and training will be provided. We hope that having a central source of information will result in considerably less confusion.

There are also some blanks on our

(40) roster of emergency shelter volunteers. We need cooks, dishwashers, and people to set up cots. Contact the town council if you can help.

Since Bob Rainey moved away, we will

(45) need one more rescue boat. Bob's partner Sarah Lightsey can train you on rescue techniques, but you will need to provide your own boat.

Thank you for pitching in to help your

(50) community. This year we can improve on our response to whatever the weather throws at us. Let's make this the safest hurricane season ever.

6. Which of the following situations is implied by lines 1–3?

(1) People did not start sandbagging early enough in previous years.
(2) Last year, the town ran out of sandbags during hurricane season.
(3) Last year, no sandbagging was done in Sea Breeze.
(4) Last year, sandbagging began as soon as a hurricane was reported.
(5) No hurricane threatened Sea Breeze last year.

7. Which of the following statements is implied in lines 18–22?

(1) In the past, Sea Breeze had no supplies during hurricane season.
(2) The town council will provide funding for increased levels of emergency supplies.
(3) In previous years, Sea Breeze had to wait for more supplies from other areas.
(4) Emergency supplies will be stockpiled at the town hall this year.
(5) In the past, Sea Breeze has distributed emergency supplies to other towns.

8. What does the passage imply about the town of Sea Breeze?

(1) The town is satisfied with its emergency response.
(2) The town wants to improve its emergency response.
(3) Hurricanes likely will be worse this year.
(4) There have been many injuries in the past.
(5) It is hit by hurricanes every year.

**Answers and explanations start on page 108.**

# Skill 5

# Get Meaning from Context

Some questions on the GED Test will ask you the meaning of a word in a passage. Often, you can figure out the meaning of an unfamiliar word by looking at the **context,** or the words and sentences that surround the word. Nearby words and phrases such as *is called, means, that is, such as,* or *for example* may be signals that the word is defined in the sentence. Other clue words and phrases such as *but, however,* or *instead of* may signal that the unfamiliar word is in contrast to or opposite in meaning to another word.

Some passages may not give specific clues like the ones mentioned above. However, you may be able to determine the meaning of an unfamiliar word from other details in the passage or from your understanding of the information or situation as a whole.

**Read the passage. Choose the <u>one best answer</u> to the question.**

These trees lent a deeper solemnity to the early light; but there was still light enough to perceive, at the farther end of this Gothic aisle, a frail reedy gig, in which were seated a young man, and by his side a young lady. Ah, young sir! What are you about? If it is requisite that you should whisper your
(5)    communications to this young lady—though really I see nobody, at an hour and on a road so solitary, likely to overhear you—is it therefore requisite that you should carry your lips forward to hers? The little carriage is creeping on at one mile an hour; and the parties within it, being thus tenderly engaged, are naturally bending down their heads. Between them and eternity, to all human
(10)   calculation, there is but a minute and a half.

Thomas De Quincey, "The English Mail Coach"

**QUESTION:** What does the word "gig" in line 2 mean?

(1) horse
(2) carriage
(3) tree
(4) shady place
(5) hut

## EXPLANATIONS

**STEP 1**  To answer this question, ask yourself:
- What is this passage about? <u>A man and a woman whispering to each other as they ride through the trees.</u>
- Are there any signal words in the context around the word? <u>The word *seated* suggests something to ride in; a "little carriage" is mentioned.</u>

**STEP 2**  Evaluate the answer choices. Which meaning <u>best</u> fits your understanding of the word?

(1) No. The people could not be seated "in" a horse.
(2) **Yes. The context indicates that a gig is something in which a man and a lady are seated, and in line 7 the words "little carriage" confirm the meaning of *gig*.**
(3) No. The context clue of the "little carriage" in line 7 makes this option incorrect.
(4) No. "Little carriage" in line 7 provides context that renders this option incorrect.
(5) No. This does not fit with the reference in line 7 to the "little carriage."

**ANSWER: (2) carriage**

## WHO IS BEING READIED FOR A CELEBRATION?

Their mahouts, who had come with them from India, and knew them as a mother knows her child, had worked on them all yesterday in the high thatched elephant-sheds among the palm-trees; crooning and clucking and slapping, washing them in the canal; painting on their foreheads, in ochre or scarlet or green, sacred symbols enlaced with elaborate scrollwork;

(5) draping their wrinkled flanks with tasseled nets brilliantly dyed and threaded with gold bullion; fastening jeweled rosettes through slits in their leather ears; grooming their tails and toes.

Mary Renault, *Funeral Games*

1. What does the word *mahouts* in line 1 mean?

   (1) Indian wise men
   (2) sacred painters
   (3) canal workers
   (4) Indian kings
   (5) elephant trainers

   **HINT**  Look for details throughout the passage that help you understand what a mahout is.

2. What does the word *ochre* in line 4 mean?

   (1) elaborate scrollwork
   (2) a color
   (3) a monster
   (4) toenails
   (5) a jeweled rosette

   **HINT**  Look at the words right before and after the unfamiliar word. What clues do they give to the meaning of the word?

## Answers and Explanations

**1. (5) elephant trainers**
Option (5) is the only choice that makes sense in context. Elephant trainers would do all of the things described in the passage.

Options (1) and (4) are not correct because nothing in the context indicates that mahouts are either wise men or kings. Option (2) is too limited and does not provide enough context; painting is only one of the many actions described in the passage. Option (3) is not correct because though "washing them in the canal" is one of the actions mentioned, that is not what canal workers do.

**2. (2) a color**
Option (2) is correct; *ochre* appears after "painting" in a list with *scarlet* and *green,* so the context indicates that ochre is another color.

Elaborate scrollwork (option 1) is mentioned later in the sentence, but the context makes it clear that the scrollwork is a different thing. Options (3) and (4) do not make sense in the context of the passage. Option (5) is mentioned later in the sentence, but the context of painting makes it clear that jeweled rosettes have nothing to do with the meaning of "ochre."

# Get Meaning from Context

**Directions: Choose the one best answer to each question.**

Questions 1 through 4 refer to the following passage.

## WHAT DOES THIS WOMAN THINK OF THE ROYAL COURT?

Nor was this splendour without varying
light and shade and gradation: the
middle distance was filled with matrons
in velvets and satins, in plumes and
(5) gems; the benches in the foreground,
to the Queen's right hand, seemed
devoted exclusively to young girls, the
flower—perhaps I should rather say, the
bud—of Villette aristocracy. Here were
(10) no jewels, no headdresses, no velvet
pile or silken sheen: purity, simplicity,
and aërial grace reigned in that virgin
band. Young heads simply braided, and
fair forms (I was going to write *sylph*
(15) forms, but that would have been quite
untrue: several of these "jeunes filles,"
who had not numbered more than
sixteen or seventeen years, boasted
contours as robust and solid as those
(20) of a stout Englishwoman of five-and-
twenty)—fair forms robed in white, or
pale rose or placid blue, suggested
thoughts of heaven and angels. I knew a
couple, at least, of these "rose et
(25) blanches" specimens of humanity.
Here was a pair of Madame Beck's late
pupils—Mademoiselles Mathilde and
Angélique: pupils, who, during their last
year at school, ought to have been in the
(30) first class, but whose brains had never
got them beyond the second division.
In English, they had been under my own
charge, and hard work it was to get them
to translate rationally a page of "The
(35) Vicar of Wakefield." Also during three
months I had one of them for my vis-
à-vis at table, and the quantity of
household bread, butter, and stewed fruit
she would habitually consume at
(40) "second déjeuner," was a real world's
wonder—to be exceeded only by the fact
of her actually pocketing slices she could
not eat. Here be truths—wholesome
truths, too.

Charlotte Brontë, *Villette*

1. What does the word *exclusively* in line 7 mean?

   (1) today
   (2) temporarily
   (3) entirely
   (4) in order
   (5) unfairly

2. What does the word *sylph* in line 14 mean?

   (1) stout
   (2) healthy
   (3) slender
   (4) proud
   (5) white

3. What does the word *vis-à-vis* in lines 36–37 mean?

   (1) waitress
   (2) student
   (3) governess
   (4) entertainer
   (5) companion

4. The narrator describes some of the young women whom she knew (lines 23–43). Which of the following best describes how the narrator feels about these young women?

   (1) They were dull and lacked manners.
   (2) They were the best and brightest students she had known.
   (3) The young women had unusually stout figures for their age.
   (4) They valued nothing but silks and velvets.
   (5) They were low-class girls who were best suited to work as maids.

Questions 5 through 8 refer to the following passage.

## HOW CAN YOU FIX YOUR COMPUTER?

### Checking Connections

Loose or improperly connected cables may cause problems for your computer, monitor, or other peripherals (such as a printer, keyboard, or mouse). To solve
(5)  these problems, check all cable connections. Make sure that each connection is tight. Then check for damaged or frayed cables. Be sure the following items are properly connected
(10)  or installed:
* the power cable
* cables to external devices

### Checking System Setup Options

Some system problems can be easily
(15)  corrected by verifying the settings for the system setup options. When you start your computer, it tries to match the system configuration information with the current hardware configuration. If the
(20)  hardware configuration doesn't match the information in the system setup options, an error message will appear on your display.

You can fix this problem by correcting
(25)  the appropriate system setup options and restarting your computer. If you have checked the system setup options and the problem persists, see Chapter 4, "Running the Powermax Diagnostics."

### (30)  Codes and Messages

Your computer can identify problems and alert you to them. When your computer identifies a problem, a message will appear on the display or
(35)  external monitor. In addition, a beep may sound.

Make a note of the message and look it up in Table 4-6. Follow the suggestions for correcting any errors.

5. What does *peripherals* in line 3 mean?

(1)  other devices that are connected to a computer
(2)  unimportant or unnecessary devices
(3)  the parts of the computer that store information
(4)  software programs
(5)  the parts of the computer that alert you to problems

6. Which word gives the best clue to the meaning of *frayed* in line 8?

(1)  connections (line 6)
(2)  tight (line 7)
(3)  damaged (line 8)
(4)  cables (line 8)
(5)  installed (line 10)

7. What does *verifying* in line 15 mean?

(1)  disconnecting
(2)  making sure something is correct
(3)  installing new equipment
(4)  registering
(5)  counting or measuring something

8. What does *Diagnostics* in line 29 mean?

(1)  a program that helps you learn how to use the computer
(2)  a glossary of computer terms
(3)  a program that finds problems with the computer
(4)  a program that helps you register your computer
(5)  a program that diagnoses medical problems

> ## TIP
>
> Context clues may be right next to an unfamiliar word or they may be several paragraphs away. Look for context clues throughout a passage to help you understand the meaning of unfamiliar words.

**Answers and explanations start on page 109.**

## Skill 6

# Apply Ideas to a New Context

The GED Test may ask you to **apply ideas to a new context.** This requires not only that you understand the meaning of words and passages, but that you apply that knowledge in a different condition or situation.

Application questions require that you change, choose, discover, identify, model, organize, select, or solve problems. You may see questions such as *What would result if…? What approach would you use…? How would you…? What does this suggest…? How do these facts support…?*

**Read the passage. Choose the <u>one best answer</u> to the question.**

### Success

Success is counted sweetest
By those who ne'er succeed.
To comprehend a nectar
Requires sorest need.

(5)  Not one of all the purple host
Who took the flag to-day
Can tell the definition
So clear, of victory,

As he, defeated, dying,
(10)  On whose forbidden ear
The distant strains of triumph
Break, agonized and clear.

Emily Dickinson

**QUESTION:** According to this poem, who would most deeply grasp the concept of health?

  (1)  a doctor practicing in a teaching hospital
  (2)  a physical education major at a university
  (3)  a patient in a chronic-care facility
  (4)  an author of educational materials on the subject
  (5)  a trained cardiovascular fitness instructor

## EXPLANATIONS

**STEP 1**  To answer this question, ask yourself:

- What is this poem about? <u>Those who do *not* have something value it and think about it the most.</u>
- How does this idea apply to the question about health? <u>A person who lacks health may focus on it more.</u>

**STEP 2**  Evaluate the answer choices. Which sentence <u>best</u> expresses the applied idea?

  (1)  No. A doctor may know much, but it is about others, not him- or herself.
  (2)  No. A physical education major may take good health for granted.
  (3)  **Yes. The person who lacks health is most keenly aware of its absence.**
  (4)  No. This is not the personal knowledge of which Dickinson speaks.
  (5)  No. This person would not long for health—he or she is healthy.

**ANSWER: (3) a patient in a chronic-care facility**

# Practice the Skill

Try these examples. Choose the one best answer to each question. Then check your answers and read the explanations.

## WHAT ARE GENRES?

One way to understand something is to categorize it. Literary works and nonfiction writing are often divided into different categories called *genres*. The genres of literary works include prose narratives, drama, and poetry. Prose narratives include short stories, novels, myths, tales, fables, and anecdotes.

(5)    The genre of a literary work may also deal with the subject matter and purpose of the piece of literature. Literary genres may take the form of mysteries, romance, or historical or science fiction, for example. Some genres are established by purpose. Literature may be informative, comic, satirical, entertaining, or persuasive.

Nonfiction genres include real-life writings such as advertising copy, almanacs, annual

(10)    reports, how-to documents, magazine articles, and letters to the editor, as well as true stories, such as personal essays, biographies, and histories.

Knowing something about different genres is a helpful way to classify different forms that you read. The more you compare what you read—no matter where you read it—with what you know, the better understanding you'll have.

---

**1.** Which of the following are examples of a nonfiction genre?

  (1) restaurant reviews
  (2) comedies
  (3) tragedies
  (4) television sitcoms
  (5) novels

**HINT** What is the definition of *nonfiction*? How does it help you to answer this question?

**2.** To which genre would an Internet blog most likely belong?

  (1) drama
  (2) mystery
  (3) short story
  (4) nonfiction essay
  (5) historical fiction

**HINT** What is an Internet blog? What kind of information does it usually contain?

---

## Answers and Explanations

**1. (1) restaurant reviews**
Option (1) is the best choice because restaurant reviews are nonfiction pieces expressing opinions about the restaurants chosen as subjects.

Option (2) is not the best choice because comedies are usually fiction. Option (3), tragedies, is also not a good choice because tragedies in literature are almost always fictional. Television sitcoms (option 4) are fiction too, as are novels (option 5) by definition, so applying them to the category of nonfiction is incorrect.

**2. (4) nonfiction essay**
Option (4) is the best choice. A blog usually consists of the thoughts of its author about things that are happening to or around him or her. Applying this idea to the concept of genre, the category that fits best is the nonfiction essay.

Option (1) is incorrect because drama is made up of plays, and few blogs, if any, are in this form. Options (2), (3), and (5) are not good choices because they are fiction; applying this term to blogs is not a good fit.

# Apply Ideas to a New Context

**Directions: Choose the one best answer to each question.**

Questions 1 through 3 refer to the following passage.

## WHAT WAS THIS VISIT LIKE?

At seven in the morning we reached Hannibal, Missouri, where my boyhood was spent. The only notion of the town that remained in my mind was the

(5) memory of it as I had known it when I first quitted it twenty-nine years ago. That picture of it was still as clear and vivid to me as a photograph.

I stepped ashore with the feeling of

(10) one who returns out of a dead-and-gone generation. I passed through the vacant streets, still seeing the town as it was, and not as it is, and finally climbed Holiday's Hill to get a comprehensive

(15) view. The whole town lay spread out below me then, and I could mark and fix every locality, every detail.

The things about me and before me made me feel like a boy again—

(20) convinced me that I was a boy again, and that I had simply been dreaming an unusually long dream. From this vantage ground, the extensive view up and down the river, and wide over the wooded

(25) expanses of Illinois, is very beautiful—one of the most beautiful on the Mississippi. It was satisfyingly beautiful to me. It had suffered no change; it was as young as ever it had been; whereas,

(30) the faces of the others would be old, and scarred with the campaigns of life, and marked with their griefs and defeats, and would give me no upliftings of spirit.

During my three days stay in the

(35) town, I woke up every morning with the impression that I was a boy—for in my dreams the faces were all young again, and looked as they had looked in the old times—but I went to bed a hundred

(40) years old, every night—for meantime I had been seeing those faces as they are now.

Mark Twain, *Life on the Mississippi*

1. What issue is the narrator struggling with that would apply in any era?

   (1) the growth of cities and towns
   (2) his regret over things he did when he was young
   (3) the loss of beauty in the environment
   (4) the way things change over time
   (5) the difference between boyhood and manhood

2. What do the narrator's dreams say about his attitude toward time?

   (1) that part of him wishes he could preserve the world as it was
   (2) that he is confused by changes in people over the years
   (3) that the past was better than the present
   (4) that he understands he wasted his youth
   (5) that aging is a natural part of life

3. What idea from this passage can a reader apply to his or her own life?

   (1) We can take comfort that people do not really change.
   (2) The present is better than memories of the past.
   (3) There is comfort in memories of childhood.
   (4) It is a bad idea to revisit scenes of one's youth.
   (5) The world changes whether we want it to or not.

## HOW SHOULD WE LIVE?

We must learn to reawaken and keep ourselves awake, not by mechanical aids, but by an infinite expectation of the dawn, which does not forsake us in our
(5)  soundest sleep. I know of no more encouraging fact than the unquestionable ability of man to elevate his life by a conscious endeavor. It is something to be able to paint a particular
(10)  picture, or to carve a statue, and so to make a few objects beautiful; but it is far more glorious to carve and paint the very atmosphere and medium through which we look, which morally we can do. To
(15)  affect the quality of the day, that is the highest of arts. Every man is tasked to make his life, even in its details, worthy of the contemplation of his most elevated and critical hour. If we refused, or rather
(20)  used up, such paltry information as we get, the oracles would distinctly inform us how this might be done.

I went to the woods because I wished to live deliberately, to front only the
(25)  essential facts of life, and see if I could not learn what it had to teach, and not, when I came to die, discover that I had not lived. I did not wish to live what was not life, living is so dear; nor did I wish
(30)  to practise resignation, unless it was quite necessary. I wanted to live deep and suck out all the marrow of life, to live so sturdily and Spartan-like as to put to rout all that was not life, to cut a broad
(35)  swath and shave close, to drive life into a corner, and reduce it to its lowest terms, and, if it proved to be mean, why then to get the whole and genuine meanness of it, and publish its meanness to the
(40)  world; or if it were sublime, to know it by experience, and be able to give a true account of it in my next excursion.

Henry David Thoreau, *Walden*

4. In lines 7–8, Thoreau speaks of the ability to "elevate" one's life by a "conscious endeavor." Applying this idea to one's own life, one would

(1) try to meet different kinds of people
(2) seek to improve one's mind
(3) improve his or her financial situation
(4) resolve never to sleep late again
(5) work harder in physical activities

5. According to the ideas in this passage, how could one die without ever having lived?

(1) by living too close to many people
(2) by not living a healthy, active life
(3) by not living in a natural environment
(4) by living without thinking much about it
(5) by dying before reaching adulthood

6. What would Thoreau most likely do if he were stuck in a job he disliked?

(1) deal with it as well as possible and do the very best he could
(2) quit and wait for something better
(3) confront his employer about the things he disliked
(4) find something to do that he cared about
(5) stop caring so much

7. What is Thoreau suggesting when he says of life that he wants "to know it by experience" (lines 40–41)?

(1) that he wants to read about as many things as possible
(2) that he must travel as much as he can
(3) that he wants every day to matter
(4) that he will understand more as he ages
(5) that he is uncertain about his beliefs

---

> **TIP**
>
> Before you can apply ideas, you must understand them. Look for the main ideas in each passage. Then think about what meaning they might have to you and the world around you.

**Answers and explanations start on page 110.**

# Skill 7

# Make Inferences

Some questions on the GED Test will ask you to make an **inference**. An inference is a conclusion that you draw by a process of reasoning. When you read a passage, you may have to infer what is meant when something is suggested but not directly stated. For example, if you read an author's description of dark clouds piling up in the western sky, you may infer that a storm is approaching.

**Read the passage. Choose the <u>one best answer</u> to the question.**

A gloomy breakfast was eaten, and the four remaining dogs were harnessed to the sled. The day was a repetition of the days that had gone before. The men toiled without speech across the face of the frozen world. The silence was unbroken save by the cries of their pursuers, that, unseen, hung upon their rear. With the coming of night in the mid-afternoon, the cries sounded closer as the pursuers drew in according to their custom; and the dogs grew excited and frightened, and were guilty of panics that tangled the traces and further depressed the two men.

Jack London, *White Fang*

**QUESTION:** Based on the passage, which of the following can you infer about the pursuers?

    (1) They are friends of the men.
    (2) They prefer warm weather.
    (3) The dogs are calmed by their presence.
    (4) They are nowhere near the men and their dogs.
    (5) They pose a threat to the men and their dogs.

## EXPLANATIONS

**STEP 1** To answer this question, ask yourself:
- What is this passage about? <u>people and animals being followed by unknown pursuers</u>
- What is the question asking me to do? <u>Use clues in the passage to determine how the men and their dogs perceive the pursuers.</u>

**STEP 2** Evaluate all of the answer choices and choose the <u>best</u> answer.

    (1) No. The passage states the men are depressed, so the pursuers are most likely not friends of the men.
    (2) No. Nothing in the passage suggests the pursuers prefer warm weather. In fact, the passage takes place in a "frozen world."
    (3) No. The passage says "the dogs grew excited and frightened, and were guilty of panics." This is not calm behavior.
    (4) No. The passage states "the cries sounded closer as the pursuers drew in," indicating the pursuers' close proximity.
    **(5) Yes. The behavior of the men and their dogs throughout the passage indicates the pursuers pose a threat to the group's wellbeing.**

**ANSWER: (5) They pose a threat to the men and their dogs.**

# Practice the Skill

Try these examples. Choose the one best answer to each question. Then check your answers and read the explanations.

## WHAT DOES HE THINK ABOUT HIS LIFE?

**Fiddler Jones:** The earth keeps some vibration going
There in your heart, and that is you.
And if the people find you can fiddle,
Why, fiddle you must, for all your life.
(5)　How could I till my forty acres
Not to speak of getting more,
With a medley of horns, bassoons and piccolos
Stirred in my brain by crows and robins
And the creak of a wind-mill—only these?
(10)　And I never started to plow in my life
That some one did not stop in the road
And take me away to a dance or picnic.
I ended up with forty acres;
I ended up with a broken fiddle—
(15)　And a broken laugh and a thousand memories,
And not a single regret.

Edgar Lee Masters, *Spoon River Anthology*

1. What inference can you make about the attitude of Fiddler Jones?

   (1) He is satisfied with his life.
   (2) He hates farming.
   (3) He resents the people who made him play his fiddle.
   (4) He regrets that he has only 40 acres.
   (5) He wishes he could play other instruments.

   **HINT** What lines in the passage address or describe Fiddler Jones's attitude?

2. What can you infer about Fiddler Jones?

   (1) He is a young man.
   (2) He is highly educated.
   (3) He is ambitious.
   (4) He is an old man.
   (5) He is bitter.

   **HINT** What details in the passage give hints about Fiddler Jones's life?

## Answers and Explanations

**1. (1) He is satisfied with his life.**
Option (1) is the best description of Fiddler Jones's attitude, which can be inferred from the final line of the passage.

Options (2) and (3) are incorrect because nothing in the passage suggests he hates farming or harbors resentment. Option (4) is not a logical inference because he says he has "not a single regret." Option (5) is not correct; he does not express a desire to play other instruments.

**2. (4) He is an old man.**
Option (4) is correct, based on the phrase "I ended up" repeated in lines 13 and 14.

Option (1) contradicts the phrase "I ended up" and the fact that he had "a thousand memories." Option (2) is not correct; nothing in the passage gives a clue about his education one way or another. Option (3) is not correct because he indicates that he has no regrets about ending up with "only" forty acres and a broken fiddle. Option (5) contradicts the final line of the passage.

# Make Inferences

**Directions: Choose the <u>one best answer</u> to each question.**

<u>Questions 1 through 4</u> refer to the following letter.

## WAS THIS CUSTOMER SATISFIED?

Dear Mr. Thompson:

 I am writing to tell you what a wonderful experience I had with your tool rental department. Last weekend, I rented a

(5) stump grinder and truck from your store. When I got home, I couldn't figure out how to loosen the strap that secured the machine in the truck. I called the store and talked to Joe. He very patiently

(10) walked me through the process, and I was able to unload the machine.

 Next, I tried to start the stump grinder. I pulled the rope, but nothing happened. I called the store again. Joe explained

(15) how to start the machine. Still, I couldn't get it started. "No problem," Joe said cheerfully. "Dave is doing some repairs in your neighborhood. He'll stop by."

 While I was waiting for Dave, I realized

(20) that I had not followed all of Joe's instructions. I felt really foolish. I tried to start the machine again, and this time the engine caught. I positioned the machine over the stump, but not much

(25) happened. By the time Dave arrived, I had not made a dent in the stump. Dave watched me for a minute. "You know," he said, "I haven't had a chance to try this new stump grinder yet. Mind if I give

(30) it a try?" He pressed a lever and the machine roared. He showed me what he had done and then said, "Now you try it." In a few minutes, my stump was just a pile of wood chips!

(35) I want you to know that both Joe and Dave went above and beyond the call of duty to help me, and they did it without making me feel foolish or incompetent. It

is my pleasure to tell you how happy I am

(40) with Handy Hardware's customer service.

Sincerely,

Linda Lopez

1. Which of the following can you infer about Mrs. Lopez from the passage?

 (1) She complains about everything.
 (2) She does a lot of yard work.
 (3) She takes pride in doing things herself.
 (4) She shops every week at Handy Hardware.
 (5) She keeps her thoughts to herself.

2. Based on the passage, which of the following can you infer about Dave?

 (1) He has been working at Handy Hardware for a long time.
 (2) He is about to get a promotion from Mr. Thompson.
 (3) He doesn't think that women should use machinery.
 (4) He is sensitive to his customers' feelings.
 (5) He is younger than Mrs. Lopez.

3. What can you infer about Joe?

 (1) He is using a cell phone.
 (2) He knows where Mrs. Lopez lives.
 (3) He has not used the stump grinder.
 (4) Dave is his best friend.
 (5) He loves his job.

4. What can you infer about the stump grinder?

 (1) It has a gas-powered engine.
 (2) It is heavy and difficult to move.
 (3) It is always problematic for customers.
 (4) Its blades are dull.
 (5) It comes in different sizes.

Questions 5 through 7 refer to the following passage.

## WHAT DID THESE PEOPLE VALUE?

What ever happened to the passion we all had to improve ourselves, live up to our potential, leave a mark on the world? Our hottest arguments were always
(5) about how we could *contribute*. We did not care about the rewards. We were young and earnest. We never kidded ourselves that we had the political gifts to reorder society or insure social
(10) justice. Beyond a basic minimum, money was not a goal we respected. Some of us suspected that money wasn't even very good for people—hence Charity's leaning toward austerity and
(15) the simple life. But we all hoped, in whatever way our capacities permitted, to define and illustrate the worthy life. With me it was always to be done in words; Sid too, though with less
(20) confidence. With Sally it was sympathy, human understanding, a tenderness toward human cussedness or frailty. And with Charity it was organization, order, action, assistance to the uncertain, and
(25) direction to the wavering.
Leave a mark on the world. Instead, the world has left marks on us. We got older. Life chastened us so that now we lie waiting to die, or walk on canes, or
(30) sit on porches where once the young juices flowed strongly, and feel old and inept and confused. In certain moods I might bleat that we were all trapped, though of course we are no more
(35) trapped than most people. And all of us, I suppose, could at least be grateful that our lives have not turned out harmful or destructive. We might even look enviable to the less lucky. I
(40) give headroom to a sort of chastened indulgence, for foolish and green and optimistic as I myself was, and lamely as I have limped the last miles of this marathon, I can't charge myself with real

(45) ill will. Nor Sally, nor Sid, nor Charity —any of the foursome. We made plenty of mistakes, but we never tripped anybody to gain an advantage, or took illegal shortcuts when no judge was
(50) around. We have all jogged and panted it out the whole way.

Wallace Stegner, *Crossing to Safety*

5. What can you infer about "the foursome," Sally, Sid, Charity, and the narrator?

   (1) They were brothers and sisters.
   (2) They had similar views on life.
   (3) The narrator is writing because the other three are ill.
   (4) They were strangers to each other.
   (5) They argued constantly.

6. Based on the passage, which of the following words best describes the narrator?

   (1) optimistic
   (2) thoughtful
   (3) shallow
   (4) envious
   (5) simple

7. Based on the passage, what can you infer about the narrator?

   (1) He is somewhat disappointed in his life.
   (2) He has accomplished a great deal.
   (3) He still plans to make important contributions.
   (4) When he was young, he thought he could reorder society.
   (5) He worries about the ill will that he once had toward others.

> **TIP**
>
> To make an inference on the GED Test, "read between the lines" to understand what an author is suggesting. Don't make a wild guess. Always be sure that there is evidence in the passage that backs up your inference.

**Answers and explanations start on page 110.**

# Skill 8

# Identify Causes and Effects

Some GED Test questions will ask you to identify cause-and-effect relationships. A **cause** is what makes something happen, while an **effect** is the result of a cause. For example, too much rain might be the cause of local flooding; the flooding is the effect of all the rain.

To find a cause, ask yourself, "Why did this happen?" To find an effect, ask, "What happened as a result?"

**Read the passage. Choose the <u>one best answer</u> to the question.**

A full hour before the party reached the city they had begun to note the perplexing changes in the atmosphere. It grew darker all the time, and upon the earth the grass seemed to grow less green. Every minute, as the train sped on, the colors of things became dingier; the fields were grown parched and yellow, the landscape hideous and bare. And along with the thickening smoke they began to notice another circumstance, a strange, pungent odor. They were not sure that it was unpleasant, this odor; some might have called it sickening, but their taste in odors was not developed, and they were only sure that it was curious. Now, sitting in the trolley car, they realized that they were on their way to the home of it—that they had traveled all from Lithuania to it.

Upton Sinclair, *The Jungle*

QUESTION: What probably caused the changes in the environment that the passage describes?

    (1) An approaching storm.
    (2) Day was turning into night.
    (3) The train was getting closer to a polluted city.
    (4) The people in the train were becoming tired.
    (5) The season was changing from summer to fall.

EXPLANATIONS

**STEP 1**

To answer this question, ask yourself:
- What is this passage about? <u>The passengers on a train approaching a city note that the environment around them is changing.</u>
- What is the question asking me to do? <u>Determine the cause of the change in environment.</u>

**STEP 2**

Evaluate the answer choices. Which sentence <u>best</u> states the cause of the changes that the passage describes?

    (1) No. Some of the changes could be caused by a storm, but most could not.
    (2) No. Some of the changes could be caused by nightfall, but most could not.
    (3) **Yes. All of the changes described, including the pollution and odor, could be caused by a city, and the first sentence mentions a city.**
    (4) No. The changes could not be caused by people becoming tired.
    (5) No. Changing seasons would not cause pollution.

ANSWER: **(3) The train was getting closer to a polluted city.**

# Practice the Skill

Try these examples. Choose the <u>one best answer</u> to each question. Then check your answers and read the explanations.

## WHAT IS BOTHERING THE SPEAKER?

True!—nervous—very, very dreadfully nervous I had been and am; but why *will* you say that I am mad? The disease had sharpened my senses—not destroyed—not dulled them. Above all was the sense of hearing acute. I heard all things in the heaven and in the earth. I heard many things in hell. How, then, am I mad? Hearken! and observe how healthily—how calmly I can tell

(5) you the whole story.

It is impossible to say how first the idea entered my brain; but once conceived, it haunted me day and night. Object there was none. Passion there was none. I loved the old man. He had never wronged me. He had never given me insult. For his gold I had no desire. I think it was his eye! yes, it was this! He had the eye of a vulture—a pale blue eye, with a film over it.

(10) Whenever it fell upon me, my blood ran cold; and so by degrees—very gradually—I made up my mind to take the life of the old man, and thus rid myself of the eye forever.

Edgar Allan Poe, "The Tell-Tale Heart"

1. Which of the following is an effect of the speaker's illness?

   (1) anger
   (2) greed
   (3) insanity
   (4) bleeding
   (5) weakness

   **HINT** What happened as a result of the speaker's illness? What did it cause?

2. What caused the speaker to decide to kill the old man?

   (1) The old man was suffering.
   (2) The old man talked too much.
   (3) The old man had insulted the speaker.
   (4) The old man had a strange-looking eye.
   (5) The old man had money that the speaker wanted.

   **HINT** What problem did the speaker have with the old man?

## Answers and Explanations

**1. (3) insanity**
Option (3) is the correct choice. The effect of the speaker's disease is insanity. In lines 1–4, the speaker questions why he is called mad, which is another term for insanity. Lines 3–4 strongly suggest that the speaker is not mentally healthy but insane.

Options (1), (4), and (5) are not supported by information in the passage, so they are not effects of the speaker's illness. Option (2) is contradicted by information in the passage, so it cannot be an effect.

**2. (4) The old man had a strange-looking eye.**
Option (4) is the correct choice. The speaker describes the eye and how it upsets him, and he decides it is a cause for murder.

Options (1) and (2) are incorrect and not supported by information in the passage. Options (3) and (5) are not correct because they are contradicted by the speaker, who says that he was never insulted by the old man and that he did not want the old man's gold.

# Identify Causes and Effects

**Directions:** Choose the **one best answer** to each question.

Questions 1 through 3 refer to the following passage.

## WHO ARE BIG EARL AND ARTHUR?

It was mid-July 1987, and Arthur was all of fourteen years old, 5'6" and 125 pounds. Big Earl tracked him down at the Delano school's scruffy, two-court
(5) playground over on Wilcox near the Expressway on Chicago's West Side. The air was filled with the buzz of cars whirring past the West Side toward the suburbs; mothers calling their children;
(10) and a half-dozen young kids, all elbows and bones and dressed in cut-offs and sweaty tanktops, shouting and playing between banged-up cars, in the streets and all around the tenements. Hovering
(15) high to the east were the skyscrapers of the business district, walls of steel and glass. Some of the players on the Delano courts could live and die in Chicago and never see the other side of the wall.
(20) But they had been playing basketball practically noon till night almost from the day they were born.

Recently Big Earl had been having doubts about scouting playground talent.
(25) He was starting to think these boys should search out other dreams. But he was in no mood to challenge the status quo, at least not today. It was dreadfully hot. And he still had some faith in the
(30) dream, and he still had dreams of his own.

Arthur was playing against guys two or three years older, and at least six inches taller. They called him "runt." In defiance,
(35) Arthur dribbled the ball from one end of the court to the other—coast to coast, as they say—through his legs, around his back, and straight up the middle. He

didn't dunk—he was too short for that—
(40) but he charged strong, drawing cheers from the kids on the edge of the court waiting for their chance to play.

Ben Joravsky, *Hoop Dreams*

1. What was the cause of Big Earl seeking Arthur at the basketball courts?

   (1) Big Earl wanted to take Arthur to see the city's skyscrapers.
   (2) Arthur's mother sent Big Earl to bring Arthur home.
   (3) Arthur had invited Big Earl to play basketball with him.
   (4) Big Earl did not like Arthur playing with the older boys.
   (5) Big Earl's job was to scout basketball players.

2. What is the most likely cause of Arthur's competing against older, taller boys?

   (1) Arthur did not have any friends his age.
   (2) The older boys forced Arthur to play with them.
   (3) Big Earl wanted to see how good Arthur really was.
   (4) Arthur was a better player than most boys his age.
   (5) Arthur did not like being called a runt.

3. Which detail from the passage describes an effect of the neighborhood's poverty?

   (1) It was very hot.
   (2) The skyscrapers had walls of steel and glass.
   (3) Big Earl still had dreams of his own.
   (4) Kids played in the streets and around the tenements.
   (5) Mothers called their children.

Questions 4 through 7 refer to the following passage.

## WHAT MAKES PEOPLE ALLERGIC TO CATS?

Having a black cat around may be bad luck after all—for those with allergies. Researchers at Long Island College Hospital have found that allergy sufferers
(5) with dark-furred cats at home reported two to four times more, and worse, symptoms than sufferers with no cats. Cat owners who allowed the animals into their bedrooms reported 19 times more
(10) symptoms. There was no statistically significant difference between patients with no cats and light-furred cats.

"I don't know why the dark cats are a problem," says Dr. Shazad Hussain, who
(15) directed the study. "It could be that they produce more sebum, which produces more of the antigens that make you sneeze." Though few allergy sufferers are willing to get rid of their pets, he says
(20) symptoms can be greatly reduced by bathing cats weekly and by keeping them away from bedrooms.

"Nothing to Sneeze At," *National Geographic*

4. What is the effect of a black cat on a person who is allergic to cats?

   (1) The person will have allergy symptoms.
   (2) The person will stop sneezing.
   (3) The person will get rid of the cat.
   (4) The person will have bad luck.
   (5) The person will need medicine.

5. What causes sneezing in people who are allergic to cats?

   (1) fur
   (2) dust
   (3) sebum
   (4) bathing
   (5) antigens

6. According to the article, researchers do not know the cause of

   (1) some people having allergies and others not
   (2) dark-furred cats causing allergy symptoms but light-furred cats not
   (3) few allergy sufferers getting rid of their cats
   (4) allergy symptoms sometimes improving
   (5) some cats liking to sleep in bedrooms

7. According to the article, what is one effect of giving a cat a weekly bath?

   (1) The cat will shed less fur.
   (2) A person with allergies will have fewer symptoms.
   (3) A person living with the cat will be less likely to develop allergies.
   (4) The cat will stay away from bedrooms.
   (5) The cat will produce more sebum.

> **TIP**
>
> Don't confuse a sequence of events with a cause-and-effect relationship. An event that happens first is not necessarily the cause of the event that happens next.

**Answers and explanations start on page 111.**

# Skill 9

# Distinguish Fact and Opinion

Some GED Test questions will ask you to **distinguish between fact and opinion**. A **fact** is a piece of information that can be proven to be true. An **opinion** is someone's belief or personal understanding of a topic. An opinion cannot be proven either true or false.

**Read the passage. Choose the <u>one best answer</u> to the question.**

Our company's projected 2008 profits are down by 30 percent from last year. Since last year's profits were the lowest in company history, this year's decline could be catastrophic. Two main factors account for the drop in profits: a decline in sales and an increase in marketing costs.

(5)       Sales are down nationwide because of decreased demand for camping gear. I think global warming is to blame, since the extreme temperatures common now may discourage people from being outdoors.

The marketing department cannot be blamed for decreased sales. In fact, the increased cost of marketing reveals the additional effort of our marketing

(10)   reps. They are making more store visits and placing more ads than ever. With sales falling, however, the return on our marketing investment is dwindling.

**QUESTION:** Which of the following is an opinion stated in the passage?

(1) Last year's profits were the lowest in company history.
(2) Two main factors account for the drop in profits.
(3) Sales are down nationwide.
(4) I think global warming is to blame.
(5) The return on our marketing investment is dwindling.

## EXPLANATIONS

**STEP 1**

To answer this question, ask yourself:
- Which of the statements can be proven true? <u>All of the statements except (4) can be proven true.</u>
- Which statement expresses the author's belief? <u>The third statement begins with "I think" and expresses the author's belief.</u>

**STEP 2**

Evaluate the answer choices. Which sentence expresses the author's opinion?

(1) No. This statement can be proven by comparing the company's profits for various years.
(2) No. This statement can be proven by analyzing the company's costs and revenues.
(3) No. This statement can be proven by analyzing sales figures.
(4) **Yes. This statement tells what the author believes about global warming's effect on demand for the company's products. It cannot be proven true or false.**
(5) No. This statement can be proven by comparing the company's current return on marketing investment to the returns for past years.

**ANSWER: (4) I think global warming is to blame.**

# Practice the Skill

Try these examples. Choose the one best answer to each question. Then check your answers and read the explanations.

## WHY PROVIDE CURBSIDE RECYCLING?

To the Editor:

Our city should provide curbside recycling for all residents. Many other cities of our size have curbside recycling. Their experience proves that more people recycle when cities make it easy to do so. In a few cities, nearly half of all trash is now recycled!

City officials have said that curbside recycling is too expensive. However, this service does (5) not have to be an added expense for the city. Some of the costs can be offset by lower costs for landfill space and maintenance. Still more costs can be offset by income from selling the newspapers, metals, and plastics that are picked up. However, studies show that such sales are not likely to completely offset the costs of the service. All city residents should pay a small fee to cover the remaining costs. I believe that some residents will object to this new (10) charge. To those who voice such an objection, I have this response: Good citizens care enough about the health of our planet to spend a few dollars to protect it.

A.Gonzalez, Garden City

1. Which sentence from the passage expresses an opinion?

   (1) Our city should provide curbside recycling for all residents.
   (2) Many other cities of our size have curbside recycling.
   (3) In a few cities, nearly half of all trash is now recycled!
   (4) Some of the costs can be offset by lower costs for landfill space and maintenance.
   (5) However, studies show that such sales are not likely to completely offset the costs of the service.

   **HINT**  Which sentence cannot be proven?

2. Which sentence from the passage is a fact?

   (1) Our city should provide curbside recycling for all residents.
   (2) City officials have said that curbside recycling is too expensive.
   (3) All city residents should pay a small fee to cover the remaining costs.
   (4) I believe that some residents will object to this new charge.
   (5) Good citizens care enough about the health of our planet to spend a few dollars to protect it.

   **HINT**  Which sentence can be proven?

---

## Answers and Explanations

**1. (1) Our city should provide curbside recycling service for all residents.**
Option (1) is the correct choice because it is the author's opinion; others may disagree.

Options (2), (3), (4), and (5) are incorrect because they are facts and can be proven to be true.

**2. (2) City officials have said that curbside recycling is too expensive.**
Option (2) is correct because it is a fact; it can be proven that city officials said this.

Options (1), (3), (4), and (5) are incorrect because they are opinions. They cannot be proven true, and others may disagree with them.

# Distinguish Fact and Opinion

**Directions: Choose the <u>one best answer</u> to each question.**

<u>Questions 1 through 3</u> refer to the following passage.

### WHO ARE THE REAL STARS?

When the Broadway version of Verdi's famous opera *Aida* opened in 2000, viewers and critics came prepared with one of two fairly predictable expectations.

(5)  Expectation #1: As in most opera productions, the singing talent will be the stars. Expectation #2: Because this much-anticipated adaptation contains new music by Sir Elton John and lyrics

(10)  by Tim Rice, the composers will be the real stars of the show. What a surprise that the real stars of *Aida* are set and costume designer Bob Crowley and lighting designer Natasha Katz. Together,

(15)  the two artists create a stage totally free of ostentation or affectation. The audience can enter the scenes without fear of stimulus overload. The viewer leaves the performance having had a

(20)  "wow" experience without the stress.

For those who expected unique results from the John/Rice collaboration, disappointment awaits you. While adequate, the music is sometimes

(25)  strident, and the lyrics are pleasant but not memorable. The performers, however, compensate for the uninspiring score. Bride-to-be Amneris (Kelly Fournier) is a Daddy's girl whose Daddy

(30)  happens to be the Pharoah. She is a charmingly self-involved clotheshorse who, by the end of the show, has developed into a legitimate and convincing princess. Her competition,

(35)  the Nubian princess Aida (Simone), is captured by the intended groom who accidentally falls in love with his victim.

Simone's deeply luscious voice by itself can win an opera audience.

(40)  However, combined with her prodigious acting skills, this artist can personally guarantee that viewers will leave happy.

It is no wonder that this adaptation has won its share of Tony Awards. If

(45)  you haven't seen *Aida* yet, adjust your expectations and get your ticket.

1. Which statement is a fact about the production discussed in the passage?

   (1)  The music is disappointing.
   (2)  The lyrics are pleasant.
   (3)  The performer who plays Amneris is convincing.
   (4)  The performer who plays Aida is outstanding.
   (5)  The production is award winning.

2. Which sentence states the author's opinion?

   (1)  The Broadway show opened in 2000.
   (2)  The production features new music.
   (3)  Two artists designed the sets, costumes, and lighting.
   (4)  The characters include two princesses.
   (5)  Everyone should see the production.

3. Which of the following best expresses the author's opinions about the composers and the set designers?

   (1)  He is impressed with the composers but not with the set designers.
   (2)  He is impressed with the set designers but not with the composers.
   (3)  He feels that the set designers were upstaged by the composers.
   (4)  He feels that both the composers and the set designers have disappointed audiences.
   (5)  He is impressed with both the composers and the set designers.

Questions 4 through 7 refer to the following passage.

## WHAT ARE THE CUTHBERTS LIKE?

Green Gables was built at the furthest edge of his cleared land and there it was to this day, barely visible from the main road along which all the other Avonlea

(5) houses were situated. Mrs. Rachel Lynde did not call living in such a place *living* at all.

"It's just *staying,* that's what," she said as she stepped along the deep-rutted,

(10) grassy lane bordered with wild rose bushes. "It's no wonder Matthew and Marilla are both a little odd, living away back here by themselves. Trees aren't much company, though dear knows if

(15) they were there'd be sure enough of them. I'd ruther look at people. To be sure, they seem contented enough; but then, I suppose they're used to it. A body can get used to anything, even to being

(20) hanged, as the Irishman said."

With this Mrs. Rachel stepped out of the lane into the backyard of Green Gables. Very green and neat and precise was that yard, set about on one side

(25) with great patriarchal willows and on the other with prim Lombardies. Not a stray stick or stone was to be seen, for Mrs. Rachel would have seen it if there had been. Privately, she was of the opinion

(30) that Marilla Cuthbert swept that yard over as often as she swept her house. One could have eaten a meal off the ground without overbrimming the proverbial peck of dirt.

L. M. Montgomery, *Anne of Green Gables*

4. Which statement is a fact that the passage reveals about Mrs. Rachel Lynde?

(1) She talks too much.
(2) She likes to be around people.
(3) She is Irish.
(4) She is a snob.
(5) She is too nosy.

5. Which statement about Green Gables is an opinion?

(1) It was built on the edge of a clearing.
(2) It was nearly hidden from the road.
(3) It was unlike the neighboring houses.
(4) It was remote and unappealing.
(5) It was surrounded by trees.

6. Mrs. Rachel thinks that the Cuthberts are

(1) strange
(2) lonely
(3) poor
(4) mean
(5) dishonest

7. Which statement best expresses Mrs. Rachel's opinion of the Cuthberts' backyard?

(1) She thinks it is too large.
(2) She thinks it is too secluded.
(3) She is impressed by its neatness.
(4) She does not like its trees.
(5) She thinks it is dirty.

> **TIP**
>
> Facts can be proven true. If you are in doubt as to whether something is a fact or an opinion, ask yourself: "Could I find absolute proof of the truth of this statement?"

**Answers and explanations start on page 112.**

# Skill 10

# Interpret Symbols and Imagery

The GED Test may ask you to **interpret symbols** and **imagery.** A symbol is something that stands for or represents something else. A symbol in writing is a word, phrase, or object that is used both for its literal meaning and to represent a broader idea. Imagery is writing that appeals to readers' senses of sight, hearing, taste, touch, or smell.

**Read the passage. Choose the <u>one best answer</u> to the question.**

### May Day

A delicate fabric of bird song
    Floats in the air,
The smell of wet wild earth
    Is everywhere.

(5)  Red small leaves of the maple
    Are clenched like a hand,
Like girls at their first communion
    The pear trees stand.

O I must pass nothing by
(10)  Without loving it much,
The raindrop try with my lips,
    The grass with my touch;

For how can I be sure
    I shall see again
(15)  The world on the first of May
    Shining after the rain?

Sara Teasdale, "May Day"

**QUESTION:** To which of the senses do lines 1 and 2 of the poem appeal?

(1) sight, taste, and smell
(2) sight, touch, and smell
(3) sight, touch, and hearing
(4) sight, hearing, and smell
(5) sight, hearing, and taste

### EXPLANATIONS

**STEP 1**

To answer this question, ask yourself:
- What imagery does the poet use in lines 1 and 2? <u>"delicate fabric," "song," and "floats"</u>
- What senses do you use to "experience" what those words describe? <u>sight, touch, and hearing</u>

**STEP 2**

Evaluate the answer choices. Which choice offers the <u>best</u> combination of senses?

(1) No. None of the words appeals to the senses of taste.
(2) No. None of the words appeals to the sense of smell.
(3) **Yes. We use touch to feel delicate fabric and sight to see it and things that float; we hear bird songs.**
(4) No. None of the words appeals to the sense of smell.
(5) No. None of the words appeals to the sense of taste.

**ANSWER: (3) sight, touch, and hearing**

# Practice the Skill

Try these examples. Choose the <u>one best answer</u> to each question. Then check your answers and read the explanations.

## FATHER AND SON

No sound—a spell—on, on out
where the wind went, our kite sent back
its thrill along the string that
sagged but sang and said, "I'm here!
I'm here!"—till broke somewhere,
gone years ago, but sailed forever clear
of earth. I hold—whatever tugs
the other end—I hold that string.

William Stafford, "Father and Son"

**1.** Which of the following best states what the string symbolizes?

(1) the lasting connection between the son and his father
(2) the commitments that tie people down
(3) the entanglements of family relationships
(4) the ideas inherited from the father
(5) the son's struggle to break free of his father

**HINT** What are strings typically used for? How could the idea of a string be related to a father and a son?

**2.** What might the kite be a symbol for in the poem?

(1) the son's hopes and dreams
(2) the love between father and son
(3) the father's failed ambitions
(4) the rivalry between father and son
(5) the business partnership between father and son

**HINT** Consider the title of the poem, and recognize that two people are flying the kite. What is the experience like?

## Answers and Explanations

**1. (1) the lasting connection between the son and his father**

Option (1) is the best choice; the string symbolizes the connection between the father and son. The son still holds the string, though not literally, that connects him to his father through the years even though both the kite and the father are gone.

Options (2), (3), and (5) are not correct because nothing in the poem supports the negative connotations related to commitments, entanglements, or a struggle. Option (4), that the string symbolizes ideas, is not suggested by the poem.

**2. (2) the love between father and son**

Option (2) is the best choice. The kite, which the two share, symbolizes their relationship. The idea is supported by the shared experience of flying the kite and the thrill of the experience.

Option (1) is not correct; the son's hopes and dreams do not fit with the idea of sharing the kite that the poem portrays. Options (3), (4), and (5) are not correct because the poem suggests nothing about ambitions, rivalry, or a business partnership.

# Interpret Symbols and Imagery

**Directions: Choose the one best answer to each question.**

Questions 1 through 4 refer to the following passage.

**WHERE IS GOODMAN BROWN GOING?**

So they parted; and the young man pursued his way until, being about to turn the corner by the meeting house, he looked back and saw the head of Faith

(5) still peeping after him with a melancholy air, in spite of her pink ribbons.

"Poor little Faith!" thought he, for his heart smote him. "What a wretch am I to leave her on such an errand! She

(10) talks of dreams, too. Methought as she spoke there was trouble in her face, as if a dream had warned her what work is to be done to-night. But no, no; 'twould kill her to think it. Well, she's a blessed angel

(15) on earth; and after this one night I'll cling to her skirts and follow her to heaven."

With this excellent resolve for the future, Goodman Brown felt himself justified in making more haste on his

(20) present evil purpose. He had taken a dreary road, darkened by all the gloomiest trees of the forest, which barely stood aside to let the narrow path creep through, and closed immediately

(25) behind. It was all as lonely as could be; and there is this peculiarity in such a solitude, that the traveler knows not who may be concealed by the innumerable trunks and thick boughs overhead; so

(30) that with lonely footsteps he may yet be passing through an unseen multitude.

Nathaniel Hawthorne, "Young Goodman Brown"

1. Goodman Brown's wife, Faith, is most likely a symbol for what idea?

   (1) civilized society
   (2) religious conviction
   (3) romantic love
   (4) selflessness
   (5) selfishness

2. To what sense do lines 20–25 appeal most?

   (1) sight
   (2) hearing
   (3) taste
   (4) touch
   (5) smell

3. What feeling does the imagery in lines 20–25 create?

   (1) a rugged sense of adventure
   (2) a growing sense of dread
   (3) a sense of rising excitement
   (4) a sense of tender privacy
   (5) a sense of serene thoughtfulness

4. What does Goodman Brown's errand most likely symbolize?

   (1) a battle against the forces of nature
   (2) a questioning of his love for his wife
   (3) the desire to be free
   (4) an exploration of uncertainty
   (5) a hope for the future

> **TIP**
>
> When you analyze imagery, find specific words that help you imagine the sights, sounds, tastes, smells, or physical sensations described in the passage.

Questions 5 through 7 refer to the following passage.

## ON WHAT SORT OF JOURNEY IS THIS MAN TRAVELING?

Going up that river was like traveling back to the earliest beginnings of the world, when vegetation rioted on the earth and the big trees were kings.
(5) An empty stream, a great silence, an impenetrable forest. The air was warm, thick, heavy, sluggish. There was no joy in the brilliance of sunshine. The long stretches of the waterway ran on, deserted,
(10) into the gloom of overshadowed distances. On silvery sandbanks hippos and alligators sunned themselves side by side. The broadening waters flowed through a mob of wooded islands; you
(15) lost your way on that river as you would in a desert, and butted all day long against shoals, trying to find the channel, till you thought yourself bewitched and cut off for ever from everything you had
(20) known once—somewhere—far away—in another existence perhaps. There were moments when one's past came back to one, as it will sometimes when you have not a moment to spare to yourself; but
(25) it came in the shape of an unrestful and noisy dream, remembered with wonder amongst the overwhelming realities of this strange world of plants, and water, and silence. And this stillness of life did
(30) not in the least resemble a peace. It was the stillness of an implacable force brooding over an inscrutable intention. It looked at you with a vengeful aspect. I got used to it afterwards; I did not see it
(35) any more; I had no time. I had to keep guessing at the channel; I had to discern, mostly by inspiration, the signs of hidden banks; I watched for sunken stones; I was learning to clap my teeth smartly before
(40) my heart flew out, when I shaved by a fluke some infernal sly old snag that would would have ripped the life out of the tin-pot steamboat and drowned all the pilgrims; I had to keep a look-out for the
(45) signs of dead wood we could cut up in the night for next day's steaming. When you have to attend to things of that sort, to the mere incidents of the surface, the reality—the reality, I tell you—fades. The
(50) inner truth is hidden—luckily, luckily. But I felt it all the same; I felt often its mysterious stillness watching me at my monkey tricks, just as it watches you fellows performing on your respective
(55) tight-ropes for—what is it? half-a-crown a tumble—

Joseph Conrad, *Heart of Darkness*

5. The writer appeals to the sense of sight with which of the following images?

   (1) "Going up that river was like traveling back to the earliest beginnings of the world . . ."
   (2) "The air was warm, thick, heavy, sluggish."
   (3) ". . . but it came in the shape of an unrestful and noisy dream . . ."
   (4) "The long stretches of the waterway ran on, deserted, into the gloom of overshadowed distances."
   (5) "And this stillness of life did not in the least resemble a peace."

6. The writer appeals to the sense of touch to convey which of the following ideas?

   (1) the length of the river
   (2) the feeling of the air
   (3) the dangers hidden in the water
   (4) the narrator's feeling of fatigue
   (5) the marvel of the sight of wild animals

7. What does the river most likely symbolize?

   (1) the difficulty of making a decision
   (2) the futility of living a good life
   (3) the journey to old age
   (4) the ancient, mysterious past
   (5) the narrator's goals for his life

**Answers and explanations start on page 112.**

## Skill 11

# Interpret Figurative Language

The GED Test may ask you to **interpret figurative language** in a sentence. Figurative language is imaginative, non-literal words and phrases used for comparison, clarity, emphasis, or style.

A **simile** makes a comparison using the words *like* or *as*.

> **Example:** He had a voice *like the low rumble of a dangerous dog*.
> The simile reveals both the sound quality and a suggestion of warning.

A **metaphor** makes a direct comparison by calling one thing another, without using the words *like* or *as*.

> **Example:** She *was a lantern in a storm* and shone brightest when it was darkest.
> The metaphor shows her ability to guide and calm others.

**Read the passage. Choose the <u>one best answer</u> to the question.**

### The Old Men Admiring Themselves in the Water

> I heard the old, old men say,
> "Everything alters,
> And one by one we drop away."
> They had hands like claws, and their knees
> Were twisted like the old thorn trees
> By the waters
> I heard the old, old men say,
> "All that's beautiful drifts away
> Like the waters."

W.B . Yeats

**QUESTION:** Yeats says the men's knees were "twisted like old thorn trees." What does this comparison show about the men?

(1) The men are no longer alive.
(2) The men are lively and still growing.
(3) The men are of no use to anyone anymore.
(4) The men are aged, stiff, and unattractive.
(5) The men are still strong and appealing.

#### EXPLANATIONS

**STEP 1**

To answer this question, ask yourself:
- What is being compared? <u>the men's legs and old thorn trees</u>
- What are the qualities of old thorn trees? <u>They are crooked, tough, knotted, inflexible, and rough looking</u>.

**STEP 2**

Evaluate the answer choices. Which sentence <u>best</u> expresses those qualities?

(1) No. The simile does not say that the trees are dead, merely that they are old.
(2) No. These ideas do not match the image of old thorn trees.
(3) No. There is no information about whether old thorn trees are useful.
(4) **Yes. To the narrator's eye, there is no physical beauty remaining in the old men.**
(5) No. This option is opposite the correct answer.

**ANSWER: (4) The men are aged, stiff, and unattractive.**

# Practice the Skill

Try these examples. Choose the one best answer to each question. Then check your answers and read the explanations.

## WHAT PLACE IS THIS?

**Have You Got a Brook in Your Little Heart?**

Have you got a brook in your little heart,
Where bashful flowers blow,
And blushing birds go down to drink,
And shadows tremble so?

(5)  And nobody knows, so still it flows,
That any brook is there;
And yet your little draught of life
Is daily drunken there.

Then look out for the little brook in March
(10)  When the rivers overflow,
And the snows come hurrying from the hills,
And the bridges often go.

And later, in August, it may be,
When the meadows parching lie,
(15)  Beware, lest this little brook of life
Some burning noon go dry!

Emily Dickinson

1. What metaphor is used in this poem?

   (1)  weather
   (2)  a flood
   (3)  seasons
   (4)  a brook
   (5)  shadows

   **HINT** Which of these choices makes a comparison to something else?

2. What does the metaphor compare to or represent in this poem?

   (1)  the way the world changes
   (2)  a person's private feelings
   (3)  a person's family
   (4)  the environment
   (5)  history

   **HINT** Which makes the most sense in the context of the poem?

---

## Answers and Explanations

**1. (4) a brook**
Option (4) is the correct choice. Dickinson uses a brook to make a comparison to something she does not name.

Options (1), (2), (3), and (5) are incorrect because they are mentioned as details and not compared to anything.

**2. (2) a person's private feelings**
Option (2) is the best choice; a brook is like a person's private feelings, which sometimes flood and sometimes go dry.

Option (1) is not the best choice because the brook represents something other than just change. Options (3), (4), and (5) are not indicated as comparisons in the poem.

# Interpret Figurative Language

**Directions: Choose the one best answer to each question.**

Questions 1 through 4 refer to the following passage.

### WHAT IS THE RABBIT DOING?

And suddenly the rabbit, which had
been crouching as if it were a flower, so
still and soft, suddenly burst into life.
Round and round the court it went, as if
(5)   shot from a gun, round and round like a
furry meteorite, in a tense hard circle
that seemed to bind their brains. They all
stood in amazement, smiling uncannily,
as if the rabbit were obeying some
(10)   unknown incantation. Round and round it
flew, on the grass under the old red walls
like a storm.
And then quite suddenly it settled
down, hobbled among the grass, and
(15)   sat considering, its nose twitching like
a bit of fluff in the wind. After having
considered for a few minutes, a soft
bunch with a black, open eye, which
perhaps was looking at them, perhaps
(20)   was not, it hobbled calmly forward and
began to nibble the grass with the mean
motion of a rabbit's quick eating.
"It's mad," said Gudrun. "It is most
decidedly mad."
(25)   He laughed.
"The question is," he said, "what is
madness? I don't suppose it is
rabbit-mad."
"Don't you think it is?" she asked
(30)   "No. That's what it is to be a rabbit."

D. H. Lawrence, *Women in Love.*

1. The rabbit crouches "as if it were a flower"
(line 2). This simile means that the rabbit

    (1)   was surprisingly visible
    (2)   sat motionless on the ground
    (3)   was likely a young one
    (4)   appeared to be dead
    (5)   was out of place in the courtyard

2. The simile "as if shot from a gun" (lines 4–5)
means that the rabbit

    (1)   ran with great speed
    (2)   was wounded
    (3)   made noise
    (4)   ran in a straight line
    (5)   was frightened

3. Which of the following phrases creates a
simile that describes the rabbit's motion?

    (1)   "round and round"
    (2)   "like a furry meteorite"
    (3)   "in a tense hard circle"
    (4)   "that seemed to bind their brains"
    (5)   "smiling uncannily"

4. The phrase "like a storm" (line 12) is a

    (1)   metaphor to hint that trouble is coming
    (2)   simile to compare the rabbit to Gudrun's
mood
    (3)   metaphor that compares fear to anger
    (4)   simple description of approaching
weather
    (5)   simile to describe the rabbit's flight

> **TIP**
>
> Remember that a simile always uses
> the words *like* or *as*. A metaphor
> directly says one thing *is* another to
> make a comparison.

Questions 5 through 10 refer to the following passage.

## WHAT WAS THIS?

### It Was Like…

It was like thunder in the mountains;
it was like mist rising from a river at
dawn; it was like a trumpet across a
campground; it was like a saxophone
(5)  playing low in a smoky jazz club; it was
like a warm wind in February; it was like
leaves blowing in a November gale; it
was like a starburst at a fireworks show;
it was like a rock-and-roll beat echoing in
(10)  my chest; it was like the summer moon
on a clear night;  it was like a sail far
across blue water; it was like a surprise
shower after drought; it was like the held
high note of a violin cadenza; it was like
(15)  driving fast the first time; it was like
sunrise over the ocean; it was like trees
bursting into bud; it was like first
snowflakes falling; it was like a candle in
a dark room; it was like the scent of
(20)  honeysuckle in May; it was like slicing
into the water from a high dive; it was
like wild geese calling from migration; it
was like standing at the edge of a cliff; it
was like lemonade on a hot day; it was
(25)  like red maples burning in autumn; it was
like the first star on a winter night; it was
like opening a perfumed letter; it was like
the drop of a falling meteor; it was like a
song from childhood; it was like a spark
(30)  shooting from a bonfire; it was like the
sound of an unseen meadowlark; it was
like neon in the night city; it was like the
smell of pine in the forest; it was like
a bell across a valley; it was like heat
(35)  lightning far away; it was like finding
something; it was like falling; it was like
feeling; it was like that, it was like that,
when you gave me that first long look
across the room, it was like that.

5. This paragraph consists almost entirely of
   which kind of figurative language?

   (1) descriptions
   (2) metaphors
   (3) sensory language
   (4) similes
   (5) quotations

6. All the figurative language in this paragraph
   is used to make a comparison to what?

   (1) the speaker's troubled past
   (2) a quest for high adventure
   (3) the future the speaker longs for
   (4) a deep feeling of romantic attraction
   (5) life's complexities and contradictions

7. The simile "like the summer moon on a clear
   night" (lines 10–11) most likely means

   (1) a feeling of cold distance
   (2) a feeling of eerie hesitation
   (3) a feeling of unimportance
   (4) a feeling of emptiness
   (5) a feeling of wonder and awe

8. The simile "like slicing into the water from a
   high dive" (lines 20–21) suggests a

   (1) rapid descent
   (2) sudden thrill
   (3) test of courage
   (4) feeling of accomplishment
   (5) loss of control

9. The simile "like neon in the night city"
   (line 32) suggests a

   (1) sense of blinding confusion
   (2) sight of unexpected threat
   (3) scene of exotic excitement
   (4) site of wasted energy
   (5) feeling of hectic annoyance

10. The simile "like the smell of pine in the
    forest" (lines 32–33) most likely means

    (1) something clean and refreshing
    (2) something sharp and stinging
    (3) something remote and lonely
    (4) something cold and forbidding
    (5) something sterile and empty

**Answers and explanations start on page 113.**

# Skill 12

# Analyze Characterization

Some questions on the GED Reading Test may ask you to analyze the way that characters are represented, or **characterized,** in a play or literary passage. Readers learn about a character through the character's thoughts, words, and actions. These thoughts, words, and actions reveal the reasons why the character behaves as he or she does. Readers can also learn about a character through the thoughts, words, and actions of other characters.

**Read the passage. Choose the <u>one best answer</u> to the question.**

Call me Ishmael. Some years ago—never mind how long precisely—having little or no money in my purse, and nothing particular to interest me on shore, I thought I would sail about a little and see the watery part of the world. It is a way I have of driving off the spleen and regulating the circulation. Whenever I find myself growing grim about the mouth; whenever it is a damp, drizzly November in my soul; whenever I find myself involuntarily pausing before coffin warehouses, and bringing up the rear of every funeral I meet; and especially whenever my hypos get such an upper hand of me, that it requires a strong moral principle to prevent me from deliberately stepping into the street, and methodically knocking people's hats off—then, I account it high time to get to sea as soon as I can.

Herman Melville, *Moby Dick*

**QUESTION:** Which of the following best describes the character of the narrator?

(1) He is a restless man who becomes impatient and moody on land.
(2) He is an ill-tempered man who has a history of getting into fights.
(3) He is a calm man who is affected more than most people by weather.
(4) He is an ill man who must go to sea for the sake of his physical health.
(5) He is a happy man who takes pleasure in the change between land and sea.

**EXPLANATIONS**

**STEP 1**  To answer this question, ask yourself:
- What is this passage about? <u>a character who goes to sea whenever he finds himself "growing grim"</u>
- What do the character's thoughts, as revealed in this passage, tell me about the character? <u>He enjoys being at sea and may even prefer it to life on land</u>

**STEP 2**  Evaluate the answer choices and choose the <u>best</u> answer.

(1) **Yes. Most of the passage describes the character's feelings when life on land begins to wear on him.**
(2) No. The passage does not say that the character fights but rather that he prevents himself from starting fights.
(3) No. The narrator mentions "damp, drizzly November" weather as a metaphor for his feelings; the phrase does not describe the actual weather.
(4) No. The narrator mentions "driving off the spleen" and "regulating the circulation" in relation to his mental state rather than to his physical health.
(5) No. The narrator describes himself as "growing grim about the mouth" and following funerals; he does not seem happy.

**ANSWER:  (1) He is a restless man who becomes impatient and moody on land.**

# Practice the Skill

Try these examples. Choose the <u>one best answer</u> to each question. Then check your answers and read the explanations.

## WHAT KIND OF PERSON IS IAGO?

> **Iago:** I follow him to serve my turn upon him:
> We cannot all be masters, nor all masters
> Cannot be truly follow'd. You shall mark
> Many a duteous and knee-crooking knave,
> (5) That, doting on his own obsequious bondage,
> Wears out his time, much like his master's ass,
> For nought but provender, and when he's old, cashier'd:
> Whip me such honest knaves. Others there are
> Who, trimm'd in forms and visages of duty,
> (10) Keep yet their hearts attending on themselves,
> And, throwing but shows of service on their lords,
> Do well thrive by them and when they have lined their coats
> Do themselves homage: these fellows have some soul;
> And such a one do I profess myself.

William Shakespeare, *Othello*

**1. What kind of character is Iago?**

(1) kind
(2) shy
(3) sneaky
(4) honest
(5) tired

> **HINT** What do the character's words reveal about him?

**2. What method of characterization is used in this passage?**

(1) other characters talk about Iago
(2) the author describes Iago
(3) we can see Iago's actions
(4) Iago describes himself
(5) none of the above

> **HINT** How do you learn about Iago?

## Answers and Explanations

**1. (3) sneaky**
Option (3) is correct. Iago says he is only following his master to "serve my turn upon him" and is "throwing but shows of service." Only a sneaky person would pretend to be loyal to someone while really plotting against him.

Options (1), (2), (4), and (5) are incorrect. Nothing in the passage suggests that Iago is kind, shy, honest, or tired.

**2. (4) Iago describes himself**
Option (4) is correct. In this speech, Iago is describing his motivations for pretending to follow his master.

Options (1) and (2) are incorrect; it is clear that no one but Iago speaks in the passage. Option (3) is incorrect because Iago is just talking, not doing anything. Option (5) is incorrect because Iago is describing himself.

# Analyze Characterization

**Directions: Choose the one best answer to each question.**

Questions 1 through 4 refer to the following passage.

## WHAT IS THE REALITY OF DON QUIXOTE?

His fancy grew full of what he used to read about in his books, enchantments, quarrels, battles, challenges, wounds, wooings, loves, agonies, and all sorts of impossible nonsense; and it so possessed his mind that the whole fabric of invention and fancy he read of was true, that to him no history in the world had more reality in it. He used to say the Cid Ruy Diaz was a very good knight, but that he was not to be compared with the Knight of the Burning Sword who with one back-stroke cut in half two fierce and monstrous giants. He thought more of Bernardo del Carpio because at Roncesvalles he slew Roland in spite of enchantments, using the technique of Hercules when he strangled Antaeus the son of Terra in his arms. He approved highly of the giant Morgante, because, although of the giant breed which is always arrogant and ill-mannered, he alone was friendly and well-bred. But above all he admired Reinaldos of Montalban, especially when he saw him sallying forth from his castle and robbing everyone he met, and when beyond the seas he stole that image of Mohammed which, as his history says, was entirely of gold. To have a bout of kicking at that traitor of a Ganelon he would have given his housekeeper and his niece into the bargain.

In short, his wits being quite gone, he hit upon the strangest notion that ever madman in this world hit upon, and that was that he fancied it was right and requisite, as well for the support of his own honour as for the service of his country, that he should make a knight-errant of himself, roaming the world over in full armour and on horseback in quest of adventures, and putting in practice himself all that he had read of as being the usual practices of knights-errant; righting every kind of wrong, and exposing himself to peril and danger from which, in the issue, he was to reap eternal renown and fame.

based on *Don Quixote de La Mancha* by Cervantes

1. What does this description of Don Quixote reveal about his mental state?

   (1) He is bitter about life's injustices.
   (2) He is envious of other men's adventures.
   (3) He is warlike and aggressive.
   (4) He is disconnected from reality.
   (5) He is fearful and suspicious.

2. What effect do the books that Don Quixote has read have on him?

   (1) They enable him to become an enchanter.
   (2) They cause him to run away with his housekeeper and his niece.
   (3) They encourage him to write his own stories.
   (4) They fill his head full of fanciful and absurd ideas.
   (5) They lead him to a life of terrible violence.

3. What kind of character is Don Quixote?

   (1) fanciful and imaginative
   (2) a writer of fantasy stories
   (3) a danger to all who know him
   (4) full of youthful ambition
   (5) isolated and lonely

4. How is Don Quixote characterized?

   (1) He describes himself.
   (2) The author describes him.
   (3) Other characters talk about him.
   (4) The reader can hear his thoughts.
   (5) The reader can see his actions.

## IS DOCTOR SLOPER AN ADMIRABLE MAN?

For a man whose trade was to keep people alive he had certainly done poorly in his own family; and a bright doctor who within three years loses his wife and
(5) his little boy should perhaps be prepared to see either his skill or his affection impugned. Our friend, however, escaped criticism; that is, he escaped all criticism but his own, which was much the most
(10) competent and most formidable. He walked under the weight of this very private censure for the rest of his days, and bore forever the scars of a castigation to which the strongest hand he knew
(15) had treated him on the night that followed his wife's death. The world, which, as I have said, appreciated him, pitied him too much to be ironical; his misfortune made him more interesting,
(20) and even helped him to be the fashion. It was observed that even medical families cannot escape the more insidious forms of disease, and that, after all, Doctor Sloper had lost other patients besides
(25) the two I have mentioned; which constituted an honorable precedent. His little girl remained to him; and though she was not what he had desired, he proposed to himself to make the best
(30) of her. He had on hand a stock of unexpended authority, by which the child, in its early years, profited largely. She had been named, as a matter of course, after her poor mother, and even
(35) in her most diminutive babyhood the doctor never called her anything but Catherine. She grew up a very robust and healthy child, and her father, as he looked at her, often said to himself that,
(40) such as she was, he at least need have no fear of losing her.

Henry James, "Washington Square"

5. How do you know how Doctor Sloper feels about himself?

The narrator says that

(1) he is a bright doctor
(2) he is determined to raise his daughter
(3) other people thought him interesting
(4) he privately criticizes himself harshly
(5) he escapes the criticism of others

6. Which of the following best describes Doctor Sloper's attitude toward his daughter?

(1) Doctor Sloper keeps his daughter out of the public eye from fear for her safety.
(2) In his grief, he hardly acknowledges his daughter's existence.
(3) He relies on other people to raise his daughter properly.
(4) Though disappointed that she is a girl, he is determined to raise her well.
(5) The child grows up wild because the doctor is preoccupied with his work.

7. What kind of man is Doctor Sloper?

(1) unforgiving
(2) frightening
(3) charming
(4) careless
(5) immature

**TIP**

Remember that you can learn about a character's inner feelings and motivations from his or her thoughts, words, and actions. You also can learn about a character from other characters' thoughts, words, and actions.

**Answers and explanations start on page 114.**

# Synthesis

## Skill 13

# Interpret Plot and Setting

Some questions on the GED Test will ask you to interpret the **plot** and **setting** of works of fiction. The plot of a story is what happens in it, and in what order. Plots usually have a beginning, middle, and end. The beginning is called the **exposition.** The exposition introduces characters, establishes the setting, and may hint at what is to come. In the middle, **complications** appear, and **conflict** arises between characters. The tension rises until the **climax,** the point of highest intensity in the story. When the conflict has been resolved, the **resolution** has been achieved at the end of the story.

The setting of a work of fiction is the place and time in which it occurs. Often, the setting of a story influences what and how things happen.

**Read the passage. Choose the <u>one best answer</u> to the question.**

Some old earthen camp or barrow, some clump of trees, at least some starved fragment of ancient hedge is usually taken advantage of in the erection of these forlorn dwellings. But, in the present case, such a kind of shelter had been disregarded. Higher Crowstairs, as the house was called, stood quite detached and undefended. The only reason for its precise situation seemed to be the crossing of two footpaths at right angles hard by, which may have crossed there and thus for a good five hundred years. Hence the house was exposed to the elements on all sides. But, though the wind up here blew unmistakably when it did blow, and the rain hit hard whenever it fell, the various weathers of the winter season were not quite so formidable on the down as they were imagined to be by dwellers on low ground.

Thomas Hardy, "The Three Strangers"

QUESTION: What is the location of the setting of "The Three Strangers"?

(1) beside an old earthen hedge by a clump of trees
(2) a fireside in a town house where the narrator tells the tale
(3) the crossing of two ancient footpaths
(4) a lone house in the high country
(5) a village called "Higher Crowstairs"

## EXPLANATIONS

**STEP 1** To answer this question, ask yourself:
- What is this passage about? <u>a house that is far up in the hills near a crossing of footpaths</u>
- What details describe the location? <u>The paragraph describes where the house is, what it's called, and how it differs from the usual houses in such areas.</u>

**STEP 2** Evaluate the answer choices. Which choice <u>best</u> describes the setting?

(1) No. The sentence says many houses sit near these features, but not this one.
(2) No. There is no suggestion of this possibility in the text.
(3) No. The footpaths are nearby, but the house is the focus of the paragraph.
**(4) Yes. The house stands by itself, away from barrow or hedge.**
(5) No. Higher Crowstairs is the name of the house. There is no village.

ANSWER: (4) a lone house in the high country

# Practice the Skill

Try these examples. Choose the <u>one best answer</u> to each question. Then check your answers and read the explanations.

## WHAT HAS HAPPENED TO THIS MAN?

When Gregor Samsa woke up one morning from unsettling dreams, he found himself changed in his bed into a monstrous vermin. He was lying on his back as hard as armor plate, and when he lifted his head a little, he saw his vaulted brown belly, sectioned by arch-shaped ribs, to whose dome the cover, about to slide off completely, could barely cling. His many legs, pitifully thin compared with the size of the rest of him, were waving helplessly before his eyes.

"What's happened to me?" he thought. It was no dream. His room, a regular human room, only a little on the small side lay quiet between the four familiar walls. Over the table, on which an unpacked line of fabric samples was all spread out—Samsa was a traveling salesman— hung the picture which he had recently cut out of a glossy magazine and lodged in a pretty gilt frame. It showed a lady done up in a fur hat and a fur boa, sitting upright and raising up against the viewer a heavy fur muff in which her whole forearm had disappeared.

Franz Kafka, *The Metamorphosis*

1. Which of the following best describes the setting of this story?

   (1) the present-day ward of a mental hospital
   (2) a hotel room such as salesman would reside in
   (3) the future in some unspecified place
   (4) the bedroom of Gregor Samsa in an unspecified time
   (5) The setting is not described.

   **HINT** What details help you to understand where and when the action occurs?

2. What complication has occurred in the beginning of this story?

   (1) Gregor Samsa is in love with a woman dressed in furs.
   (2) Gregor Samsa has been transformed into an insect.
   (3) Gregor Samsa dreams he has been changed into an insect.
   (4) Gregor Samsa has been troubled by unsettling dreams.
   (5) Gregor Samsa has lost his job as a salesman.

   **HINT** What problem or issue must be resolved?

---

## Answers and Explanations

**1. (4) the bedroom of Gregor Samsa in an unspecified time**

Option (4) is correct. The room where this strange event has occurred is Gregor's room, at some time in the past.

Option (1) is incorrect because there is no indication within the passage that the setting is a mental ward. Option (2) is not correct because the text says it is his room with its "four familiar walls." Option (3) is incorrect because nothing in the passage suggests that the story is set in the future. Option (5) is not correct because the text does supply information about the setting.

**2. (2) Gregor Samsa has been transformed into an insect.**

Option (2) is correct. This stunning and famous opening introduces the character, a complication, and a conflict in a single sentence.

Options (1) and (5) are incorrect because there is nothing in the text to indicate Samsa is in love with the woman or has lost his job. Option (3) is incorrect because the text says plainly, "It was no dream." Option (4) is incorrect because the dreams are not the complication; the transformation into a giant insect is.

# Interpret Plot and Setting

**Directions: Choose the one best answer to each question.**

Questions 1 through 4 refer to the following passage.

## WHAT WILL BARTLEBY DO?

"I have given up copying," he answered, and slid aside.

He remained as ever, a fixture in my chamber. Nay—if that were possible—he
(5) became still more of a fixture than before. What was to be done? He would do nothing in the office; why should he stay there? In plain fact, he had now become a millstone to me, not only useless as a
(10) necklace, but afflictive to bear. Yet I was sorry for him. I speak less than truth when I say that, on his own account, he occasioned me uneasiness. If he would but have named a single relative or friend,
(15) I would instantly have written, and urged their taking the poor fellow away to some convenient retreat. But he seemed alone, absolutely alone in the universe. A bit of a wreck in the mid-Atlantic. At length,
(20) necessities connected with my business tyrannized over all other considerations. Decently as I could, I told Bartleby that in six days' time he must unconditionally leave the office. I warned him to take
(25) measures, in the interval, for procuring some other abode. I offered to assist him in this endeavor, if he himself would but take the first step towards a removal. "And when you finally quit me, Bartleby,"
(30) added I, "I shall see that you go not away entirely unprovided. Six days from this hour, remember."

Herman Melville, "Bartleby the Scrivener"

1. What is the location of the setting?

   (1) the narrator's office
   (2) the home of one of Bartleby's relatives
   (3) a cabin in a ship in the mid-Atlantic
   (4) Bartleby's home
   (5) the narrator's home

2. Which of the following best describes the time period in which the story takes place?

   (1) the ancient past
   (2) just after World War II
   (3) six days ago
   (4) the past
   (5) the present

3. Based on this passage, what is the conflict taking place in the story?

   (1) The narrator needs the copying to be continued.
   (2) Bartleby will not leave the narrator's office.
   (3) Bartleby fears to return to the sea.
   (4) Bartleby has been stealing from the narrator.
   (5) The narrator's business is failing.

4. How does Bartleby occupy his time?

   (1) He does nothing.
   (2) He copies documents.
   (3) He works at the mill.
   (4) He does general office work.
   (5) He writes letters.

[ **TIP** ]

The general setting is often the easiest thing to find in a story. Then look for details to fine-tune your understanding. Watch for ways that setting influences plot or influences actions that take place.

## WHAT WILL HAPPEN?

**Juliet:** What man art thou that, thus bescreened in night,
So stumblest on my counsel?
**Romeo:** By a name
(5) I know not how to tell thee who I am.
My name, dear saint, is hateful to myself,
Because it is an enemy to thee.
Had I it written, I would tear the word.
(10) **Juliet:** My ears have yet not drunk a hundred words
Of thy tongue's uttering, yet I know the sound.
Art thou not Romeo, and a Montague?
(15) **Romeo:** Never, fair maid, if either thee dislike.
**Juliet:** How camest thou hither, tell me, and wherefore?
The orchard walls are high and hard to climb,
(20) And the place death, considering who thou art,
If any of my kinsmen find thee here.
**Romeo:** With love's light wings did I
(25) o'erperch these walls;
For stony limits cannot hold love out,
And what love can do, that dares love attempt.
Therefore thy kinsmen are no stop
(30) to me.
**Juliet:** If they do see thee, they will murder thee.
**Romeo:** Alack, there lies more peril in thine eye
(35) Than twenty of their swords! Look thou but sweet,
And I am proof against their enmity.
**Juliet:** I would not for the world they saw thee here.
(40) **Romeo:** I have night's cloak to hide me from their eyes;
And but thou love me, let them find me here.
My life were better ended by their hate
(45) Than death proroguèd, wanting of thy love.

**Juliet:** By whose direction found'st thou out this place?
**Romeo:** By love, that first did prompt
(50) me to inquire.
He lent me counsel, and I lent him eyes.
I am no pilot; yet, wert thou as far
As that vast shore washed with the
(55) farthest sea,
I should adventure for such merchandise.
**Juliet:** Thou knowest the mask of night is on my face;
(60) Else would a maiden blush bepaint my cheek
For that which thou hast heard me speak to-night.
Fain would I dwell on form—fain,
(65) fain deny
What I have spoke; but farewell compliment!
Dost thou love me? I know thou wilt say 'Ay';
(70) And I will take thy word. Yet, if thou swear'st,
Thou Mayst prove false. At lovers' perjuries,
They say Jove laughs.

William Shakespeare, *Romeo and Juliet*

5. What is the physical setting of this scene?

   (1) a forest at night
   (2) a city street at dusk
   (3) outside the walls of an orchard
   (4) daybreak on the walls of a castle
   (5) inside a courtyard at night

6. What conflict is revealed in this scene?

   (1) Romeo is in love with Juliet.
   (2) Juliet hates Romeo.
   (3) Juliet's family wants to kill Romeo.
   (4) Romeo can't get past the walls.
   (5) Juliet doesn't know who is speaking.

**Answers and explanations start on page 114.**

# Skill 14

# Analyze Word Choice

Some GED Test questions will ask you to **analyze word choice** in passages you read. Writers choose their words carefully, selecting words with just the right shades of meaning. Writers pay attention not only to what each word **denotes**—its definition—but also to the word's **connotation**—the feelings and ideas associated with it.

**Read the passage. Choose the <u>one best answer</u> to the question.**

A few weeks ago I went into our little downtown restaurant and saw that it had replaced its tired old salad bar with a gorgeous saltwater aquarium with sea anemones, chunks of living coral, and big slow-moving colorful fish with faces I could almost recognize. I spent my whole lunchtime staring into that tank, mesmerized
(5) by the fish as they gracefully looped and glided, sending the tentacles of the sea anemones into slow twirls and fanning out the tall grasses.

When I finished my sandwich I noticed that there were a couple of crumbs left on my plate, just right to pinch between thumb and finger. Oh, I thought, to pinch up those crumbs and dip my fingers down into the water, breaking through the smooth
(10) surface into the coolness and silence of that peaceful world. One of the fish would make a looping turn, his odd exophthalmic eyes would rotate slowly in their sockets and fix upon the crumbs in my fingers. Then he would angle up, and I would feel for just one exquisite instant those thorny fishy lips rasping across my fingertips. With rising delight and anticipation, I pinched up a crumb, two crumbs. I scrabbled across
(15) the plastic top of the tank, found the little door, lifted it open—and then I saw the sign: DO NOT FEED THE FISH.

Bailey White, *Sleeping at the Starlight Motel*

**QUESTION:** In line 13, the words *thorny* and *rasping* show that the fish is

(1) hungry
(2) dangerous
(3) large
(4) strange looking
(5) rough skinned

## EXPLANATIONS

**STEP 1**

To answer this question, ask yourself:
- What is this part of the passage describing? <u>what it would feel like to touch the fish</u>
- What do the words describe? <u>the texture of the fish's skin</u>

**STEP 2**

Evaluate the answer choices. Which choice <u>best</u> expresses what the author meant to convey with the words *thorny* and *rasping*?

(1) No. The words *thorny* and *rasping* do not describe hunger.
(2) No. The author did not think the fish were dangerous.
(3) No. The words *thorny* and *rasping* do not describe the size of the fish.
(4) No. This part of the passage is not describing how the fish looks.
(5) **Yes. In line 13, the author is describing how the fish's mouth would feel to him if it touched him.**

**ANSWER: (5) rough skinned**

# Practice the Skill

Try these examples. Choose the <u>one best answer</u> to each question. Then check your answers and read the explanations.

## WILL HE FOLLOW THE PATH TO TRUTH?

### The Wayfarer

The wayfarer,
Perceiving the pathway to truth,
Was struck with astonishment.
It was thickly grown with weeds.
(5)   "Ha," he said,
"I see that none has passed here
In a long time."
Later he saw that each weed
Was a singular knife.
(10)   "Well," he mumbled at last,
"Doubtless there are other roads."

Stephen Crane, "The Wayfarer"

1. Which word would be the best choice to replace the word *wayfarer* in the title and first line of the poem?

   (1)  traveler
   (2)  visitor
   (3)  commuter
   (4)  tourist
   (5)  pedestrian

   **HINT**  What kind of person is described in the poem?

2. The poet's choices of the word *said* in line 5 and the word *mumbled* in line 10 show that the wayfarer

   (1)  became angry at the obstacles
   (2)  grew increasingly proud of his efforts
   (3)  doubled his effort as it got harder
   (4)  lost his resolve as the way grew hard
   (5)  grew wiser as he progressed down the path

   **HINT**  Which answer choice describes a person who would be likely to mumble?

---

## Answers and Explanations

**1. (1) traveler**
Option (1) is the correct choice. *Traveler* has nearly the same meaning as *wayfarer*. In the poem, a travelor might consider one path before deciding to look for other roads.

Option (2) is not the best choice because *visitor* does not suggest the sense of wandering that *wayfarer* does. Option (3) is incorrect because the wayfarer is not going back and forth to work. Option (4) is incorrect because the wayfarer is not merely sightseeing, and option (5) is not correct because *wayfarer* suggests more than merely a walker.

**2. (4) lost his resolve as the way grew hard**
Option (4) is the correct choice. The change in words shows that the wayfarer gave up and made excuses. *Said* conveys more confidence, but *mumbled* connotes uncertainty, shame, or timidity.

Options (1) (2), (3), and (5) are incorrect. The word *mumbled* does not connote anger, pride, resolve, or wisdom.

# Analyze Word Choice

**Directions:** Choose the <u>one best answer</u> to each question.

<u>Questions 1 through 4</u> refer to the following passage.

## WHO IS MRS. DALLOWAY?

How much she wanted it—that people should look pleased as she came in, Clarissa thought and turned and walked back towards Bond Street, annoyed,

(5) because it was silly to have other reasons for doing things. Much rather would she have been one of those people like Richard who did things for themselves, whereas, she thought,

(10) waiting to cross, half the time she did things not simply, not for themselves; but to make people think this or that; perfect idiocy she knew (and now the policeman held up his hand) for no one was ever

(15) for a second taken in. Oh if she could have had her life over again! she thought, stepping on to the pavement, could have looked even differently!

She would have been, in the first

(20) place, dark like Lady Bexborough, with a skin of crumpled leather and beautiful eyes. She would have been, like Lady Bexborough, slow and stately; rather large; interested in politics like a man;

(25) with a country house; very dignified, very sincere. Instead of which she had a narrow pea-stick figure; a ridiculous little face, beaked like a bird's. That she held herself well was true; and had nice hands

(30) and feet; and dressed well, considering that she spent little. But often now this body she wore (she stopped to look at a Dutch picture), this body, with all its capacities, seemed nothing—nothing at

(35) all. She had the oddest sense of being herself invisible; unseen; unknown; there being no more marrying, no more having children now, but only this astonishing and rather solemn progress with the rest

(40) of them, up Bond Street, this being Mrs. Dalloway; not even Clarissa any more; this being Mrs. Richard Dalloway.

Virginia Woolf, *Mrs. Dalloway*

1. The author's choice of the word *idiocy* in line 13 shows that Mrs. Dalloway

   (1) makes excuses for her behavior
   (2) judges herself harshly
   (3) accepts herself as she is
   (4) is proud of herself
   (5) is unaware of how others see her

2. The phrase *crumpled leather* in line 21 conveys that Lady Bexborough's face is

   (1) weathered
   (2) fat
   (3) beautiful
   (4) pale
   (5) friendly

3. Which word would be the best choice to replace *annoyed* in line 4?

   (1) enraged
   (2) angry
   (3) irritated
   (4) furious
   (5) anxious

4. The words "invisible; unseen; unknown" in line 36 all have similar meanings. What does the author achieve by using all three words instead of just one word?

   (1) The author makes the passage easier for readers to understand.
   (2) The author implies that Mrs. Dalloway is insane.
   (3) The author describes Mrs. Dalloway as three different people see her.
   (4) The author emphasizes that Mrs. Dalloway feels she has little identity or existence.
   (5) The author hints that Mrs. Dalloway is behaving suspiciously.

Questions 5 through 8 refer to the following passage.

## WHY IS THIS WOMAN UNHAPPY?

He ushered her into a slip of a hall hung with old prints. She noticed the letters and notes heaped on the table among his gloves and sticks; then she
(5) found herself in a small library, dark but cheerful, with its walls of books, a pleasantly faded Turkey rug, a littered desk, and as he had foretold, a tea-tray on a low table near the window. A
(10) breeze had sprung up, swaying inward the muslin curtains and bringing a fresh scent of mignonette and petunias from the flower-box on the balcony.

Lily sank with a sigh into one of the
(15) shabby leather chairs.

"How delicious to have a place like this all to one's self! What a miserable thing it is to be a woman." She leaned back in a luxury of discontent.

(20) Selden was rummaging in a cupboard for the cake.

"Even women," he said, "have been known to enjoy the privileges of a flat."

"Oh, governesses—or widows. But not
(25) girls—not poor, miserable, marriageable girls!"

"I even know a girl who lives in a flat." She sat up in surprise. "You do?"

"I do," he assured her, emerging from
(30) the cupboard with the sought-after cake.

"Oh, I know—you mean Gerty Farish." She smiled a little unkindly. "But I said *marriageable*—and besides, she has a horrid little place, and no maid, and such
(35) queer things to eat. Her cook does the washing and the food tastes of soap. I should hate that, you know."

"You shouldn't dine with her on washdays," said Selden, cutting the
(40) cake.

They both laughed, and he knelt by the table to light the lamp under the kettle, while she measured out the tea into a little tea-pot of green glaze. As he
(45) watched her hand, polished as a bit of old ivory, with its slender pink nails and the sapphire bracelet slipping over her wrist, he was struck with the irony of suggesting to her such a life as his
(50) cousin Gertrude Farish had chosen. She was so evidently the victim of the civilization which had produced her that the links of her bracelet seemed like manacles chaining her to her fate.

Edith Wharton, *The House of Mirth*

5. What does the author mean by "a luxury of discontent" in lines 18–19?

(1) Lily is uncomfortable in Selden's apartment.
(2) Lily enjoys complaining about her life.
(3) Lily is only happy when she has the finest things.
(4) Lily has never liked Selden.
(5) Lily hates being poor.

6. The word *slip* in line 1 conveys that the hall was

(1) slick
(2) hidden
(3) dark
(4) depressing
(5) small

7. Which word could best replace *scent* in line 12?

(1) smell
(2) stench
(3) aroma
(4) odor
(5) stink

8. Which words in the last sentence of the passage best convey Lily's powerlessness?

(1) evidently, civilization
(2) civilization, produced
(3) links, bracelet
(4) victim, fate
(5) bracelet, seemed

**Answers and explanations start on page 115.**

---

TIP

To analyze an author's choice of words, try replacing the word in question with a word that has a similar meaning. Ask yourself how the feel of the passage changes.

# Skill 15

# Draw Conclusions

When you read, you put together details and facts in the text and **draw conclusions** about events, characters, or information. For example, if you read about a character who will stop at nothing to acquire wealth, you may draw the conclusion that he is greedy. By putting details and facts together and drawing logical conclusions from them, you better understand what you are reading.

Some questions on the GED Reading Test may ask you to draw conclusions. Make sure that the conclusions you draw are based on evidence in the text. You should be able to use details and facts from the text to explain the conclusions that you draw.

**Read the passage. Choose the <u>one best answer</u> to the question.**

### With Rue My Heart Is Laden

With rue my heart is laden
For golden friends I had,
For many a rose-lipped maiden
And many a lightfoot lad.

(5)　By brooks too broad for leaping
The lightfoot boys are laid;
The rose-lipped girls are sleeping
In fields where roses fade.

A. E. Housman, "With Rue My Heart Is Laden"

**QUESTION:** What conclusion can you draw about the "lightfoot boys" and the "rose-lipped girls"?

(1) They are dead and buried.
(2) The narrator never knew them.
(3) The narrator had a falling-out with them.
(4) The boys and girls were married to each other.
(5) The boys and girls were the narrator's brothers and sisters.

**EXPLANATIONS**

**STEP 1**　To answer this question, ask yourself:
- What details does the poem include about the "lightfoot boys" and the "rose-lipped girls"? <u>The boys are laid by brooks and the girls are sleeping in fields.</u>
- What can I conclude from these details? <u>The boys and girls have died and are buried beside brooks and in fields.</u>

**STEP 2**　Evaluate the answer choices. Which sentence <u>best</u> expresses a logical conclusion?

(1) **Yes. This choice is the logical conclusion based on the statements that the boys "are laid" by brooks and the girls "are sleeping" in fields.**
(2) No. This is not correct; line 2 refers to them as "friends I had."
(3) No. No details in the poem suggest this conclusion.
(4) No. No details in the poem suggest this conclusion.
(5) No. This is not correct because the narrator calls them "friends" in line 2.

**ANSWER: (1) They are dead and buried.**

# Practice the Skill

Try these examples. Choose the **one best answer** to each question. Then check your answers and read the explanations.

## HOW CAN PARENTS HELP CHILDREN WITH THEIR HOMEWORK?

Here are some suggestions for parents who help their children with homework:

- Designate a comfortable, well-lit, quiet place for doing homework.
- Take breaks. Children often have shorter attention spans than you would think. Here's a good formula: Add five to the child's age. Expect the child to be able to work for that

(5)    many minutes without a break.

- If you have more than one child to help, help each one separately so that your attention is not divided.
- Help, but don't do the work yourself. Instead, reword questions to help your child understand them, or help the child outline the steps to working through a problem.

(10)    Remember that you're *helping*, not *doing* the homework.

1. What conclusion can you draw from this?

  (1)  Children need to be pushed to complete their homework.
  (2)  Children rarely can figure things out for themselves.
  (3)  Children should do as much of their homework as they can on their own.
  (4)  Children have excellent powers of concentration.
  (5)  Children do not benefit from parents' attention when doing their homework.

**HINT** Consider the details in the passage. What do they "add up" to?

2. According to the passage, which of the following would be a good place to do homework?

  (1)  on a sofa with the television playing quietly
  (2)  at a table in a bright room where other children are playing
  (3)  on the bus on the way home from school
  (4)  at the kitchen table while a meal is being prepared
  (5)  at a desk with a lamp and a chair in an out-of-the-way room

**HINT** A conclusion must be based on facts or details in a passage. Don't make unsupported assumptions.

## Answers and Explanations

**1. (3) Children should do as much of their homework as they can on their own.**

Option (3) is a logical conclusion based on the details in lines 8–10 of the passage.

Option (1) is not correct because the passage does not discuss children's willingness to do homework. Option (2) is incorrect. The passage does not suggest this. Option (4) contradicts the information in lines 3–5. Option (5) contradicts the main idea of article, and specifically contradicts lines 6–7.

**2. (5) at a desk with a lamp and a chair in an out-of-the-way room**

Option (5) is the best choice; it describes a place that is comfortable, well-lit, and quiet, as recommended in line 2.

Option (1) is not logical because the criteria call for a quiet place, but a television would be a distraction. Option (2) is not correct because a room where children are playing would not be quiet. Option (3) would be neither quiet nor comfortable. Option (4) would likely not be quiet, and the parents' attention would be divided between helping with the homework and preparing the meal.

# Draw Conclusions

**Directions: Choose the one best answer to each question.**

Questions 1 through 3 refer to the following passage.

### SHOULD CAESAR BE AFRAID?

**Brutus:** .... But look you, Cassius,
The angry spot doth glow on Caesar's
brow,
And all the rest look like a chidden train.
(5)  Calpurnia's cheek is pale, and Cicero
Looks with such ferret and such fiery
eyes
As we have seen him in the Capitol,
Being crossed in conference by some
(10)  senators.
**Cassius:** Casca will tell us what the
matter is.
**Caesar:** Antonius.
**Antony:** Caesar?
(15) **Caesar:** Let me have men about me that
are fat,
Sleek-headed men, and such as sleep
a-nights.
Yond Cassius has a lean and hungry
(20)  look;
He thinks too much: such men are
dangerous.
**Antony:** Fear him not, Caesar, he's not
dangerous;
(25)  He is a noble Roman, and well given.
**Caesar:** Would he were fatter! But I fear
him not.
Yet if my name were liable to fear,
I do not know the man I should avoid
(30)  So soon as that spare Cassius. He reads
much,
He is a great observer, and he looks
Quite through the deeds of men. He
loves no plays,
(35)  As thou dost Antony; he hears no music;
Seldom he smiles, and smiles in such
a sort

As if he mocked himself, and scorned
his spirit
(40)  That could be moved to smile at
anything.
Such men as he be never at heart's ease
Whiles they behold a greater than
themselves,
(45)  And therefore are they very dangerous.
I rather tell thee what is to be feared
Than what I fear; for always I am Caesar.
Come on my right hand, for this ear
is deaf,
(50)  And tell me truly what thou think'st
of him.

William Shakespeare, *Julius Caesar*

1. What do Caesar's comments suggest about his character?

   (1)  He is proud and confident.
   (2)  He is self-conscious about his deafness.
   (3)  He is a timid ruler who trusts no one.
   (4)  He has a suspicious nature that sees treachery on all sides.
   (5)  He is a poor judge of character.

2. What can you conclude based on lines 15–22?

   (1)  Caesar thinks Cassius is unattractive.
   (2)  Caesar is suspicious of Cassius.
   (3)  Caesar dislikes Cassius because he is bald.
   (4)  Caesar has heard that Cassius suffers from insomnia.
   (5)  Caesar does not like intelligent men.

3. What conclusion can you draw about Antony, based on the passage?

   (1)  He is plotting with Cassius.
   (2)  He is liable to tell Caesar anything just to stay in his favor.
   (3)  He is fond of plays and music.
   (4)  He is fat and resents Caesar's comments.
   (5)  He is only slightly acquainted with Caesar.

Questions 4 and 5 refer to the following passage.

## WHAT WILL HAPPEN BETWEEN THIS COUPLE?

Never did I dance more lightly. I felt myself more than mortal, holding this loveliest of creatures in my arms, flying, with her as rapidly as the wind, till I

(5) lost sight of every other object; and O Wilhelm, I vowed at that moment, that a maiden whom I loved, or for whom I felt the slightest attachment, never, never should waltz with any one else but with

(10) me, if I went to perdition for it!—you will understand this.

We took a few turns in the room to recover our breath. Charlotte sat down, and felt refreshed by partaking of some

(15) oranges which I had had secured,—the only ones that had been left; but at every slice which, from politeness, she offered to her neighbours, I felt as though a dagger went through my heart.

(20) We were the second couple in the third country dance. As we were going down (and Heaven knows with what ecstasy I gazed at her arms and eyes, beaming with the sweetest feeling of pure and

(25) genuine enjoyment), we passed a lady whom I had noticed for her charming expression of countenance; although she was no longer young. She looked at Charlotte with a smile, then, holding

(30) up her finger in a threatening attitude, repeated twice in a very significant tone of voice the name of "Albert."

"Who is Albert," said I to Charlotte, "if it is not impertinent to ask?" She was

(35) about to answer, when we were obliged to separate, in order to execute a figure in the dance; and, as we crossed over again in front of each other, I perceived she looked somewhat pensive. "Why

(40) need I conceal it from you?" she said, as she gave me her hand for the promenade. "Albert is a worthy man, to whom I am engaged." Now, there was

nothing new to me in this (for the

(45) girls had told me of it on the way); but it was so far new that I had not thought of it in connection with her whom, in so short a time, I had learned to prize so highly. Enough, I became confused,

(50) got out in the figure, and occasioned general confusion; so that it required all Charlotte's presence of mind to set me right by pulling and pushing me into my proper place.

J. W. von Goethe, *The Sorrows of Young Werther*

4. Which of the following is a logical conclusion based on the first paragraph (lines 1–11)?

(1) The narrator is dancing with a woman he has known for a long time.
(2) The narrator is blind.
(3) The narrator is an excellent dancer.
(4) The narrator has fallen in love.
(5) This is the narrator's first waltz with this partner.

5. What conclusion can you draw about Charlotte?

(1) She enjoys dancing.
(2) She is secretly married.
(3) She is the daughter of the woman who said "Albert."
(4) She is a liar.
(5) She is in love with the narrator.

> **TIP**
>
> Any conclusion you draw from a passage must be based on details and facts given in the passage. A conclusion must be logical; it should not be a wild guess.

**Answers and explanations start on page 115.**

## Skill 16

# Interpret Overall Style and Structure

Some questions on the GED Reading Test may ask you to interpret the **style** or **structure** of a piece of writing. Style refers to the words authors choose and how they use those words. The style of a passage is formal if the words are standard English and the sentences are complete and correct. An informal style is more casual and may use slang, colloquial expressions, and sentence fragments. The style of a piece of writing also may be humorous or serious, simple or complex.

Structure refers to the way in which an author organizes the writing. Fiction can be organized in chronological order, or an author may present events out of order to create suspense. Nonfiction is organized in various ways, such as around a main idea and supporting details, around comparisons and contrasts, or according to cause and effect.

**Read the passage. Choose the one best answer to the question.**

At the 2008 Olympic games, Cullen Jones was a part of the gold-medal winning 4 × 100 freestyle relay. He is only the third African American to compete in swimming for the United States in the Olympics and is the first African American ever to hold a swimming world record. The sport of swimming may never have had this star if not for a near tragedy 19 years earlier.

When Jones was only 5, he nearly drowned at a water park he was visiting with his family. Rescued by lifeguards, Jones knew the only way to avoid danger in the future was to learn how to swim properly. Now an Olympic gold-medalist, Jones spends his free time teaching other minority children how to swim in the hopes he can help them avoid the dangers of drowning, too.

**QUESTION:** Which of the following best describes the overall structure of this passage?

(1) The author tells events in time order.
(2) The author describes an effect and then reveals the cause.
(3) The author presents one main idea and many supporting details.
(4) The author states an opinion and gives reasons that support the opinion.
(5) The author asks a question and then answers it.

**EXPLANATIONS**

**STEP 1** To answer this question, ask yourself:
- What kind of writing is this—fiction or nonfiction? <u>nonfiction</u>
- How is the passage organized? <u>It describes an accomplishment and then tells the reason behind the accomplishment.</u>

**STEP 2** Evaluate the answer choices. Which sentence <u>best</u> describes the structure of the passage?

(1) No. First the author describes Jones's 2008 Olympic accomplishment; then he talks about what happened to Jones when he was 5.
(2) **Yes. Jones's swimming skills described in the first paragraph are the result of him learning how to swim properly after he nearly drowned, which is described in the second paragraph.**
(3) No. This passage does not present a main idea and then support it.
(4) No. The passage does not express an opinion.
(5) No. The passage does not ask a question.

**ANSWER: (2) The author describes an effect and then reveals the cause.**

# Practice the Skill

Try these examples. Choose the <u>one best answer</u> to each question. Then check your answers and read the explanations.

## WHAT CHANGES COME WITH SPRING?

### SPRING IS LIKE A PERHAPS HAND

Spring is like a perhaps hand
(which comes carefully
out of Nowhere)arranging
a window,into which people look(while
(5)    people stare
arranging and changing placing
carefully there a strange
thing and a known thing here)and

changing everything carefully

(10)   spring is like a perhaps
Hand in a window
(carefully to
and fro moving New and
Old things, while
(15)   people stare carefully
moving a perhaps
fraction of flower here placing
an inch of air there) and

without breaking anything.

e. e. cummings, "Spring Is Like a Perhaps Hand"

1. Which word best describes the style of the poem?

   (1) formal
   (2) serious
   (3) original
   (4) simple
   (5) predictable

   **HINT** How would you describe the poem?

2. Which of these methods of organization gives structure to the poem?

   (1) rhyme
   (2) repetition
   (3) time order
   (4) cause and effect
   (5) narrative

   **HINT** How would you describe the organization?

---

## Answers and Explanations

**1. (3) original**
Option (3) is the correct choice because the poem's sentences use unexpected, disjointed word order and unusual line breaks and spacings.

Options (1), (2), (4), and (5) are incorrect; the words and sentences in the poem are not formal, serious, simple, or predictable.

**2. (2) repetition**
Option (2) is the correct choice; several elements are repeated in the poem, including "spring is like a perhaps hand."

Options (1), (3), (4), and (5) are incorrect because the poem is not organized according to rhyme, time order, cause and effect, or conventional narrative.

*Skill 16: Interpret Overall Style and Structure* **71**

# Interpret Overall Style and Structure

**Directions: Choose the one best answer to each question.**

Questions 1 through 4 refer to the following passage.

## IS SHE REALLY INTERESTED IN HER BROTHER?

I tell you, Bernie, it is my business, what my own brother does. Hasn't he been here nearly four months and never paid a penny of rent, not even a

(5) five-pound note to buy something for myself, and him rolling in it, ten thousand pounds he has, if he has a penny. I tell you he has more money than he lets on, the least he might do is think of his

(10) sister, his nearest and dearest relative on this side of the ocean and not some old spinster woman that probably has plenty, a lady of leisure, if you please. If you think of all the dinners he's eaten

(15) here and never asked me if I had a mouth on me. No, that's not the point, I will not get rid of him, he's my own brother and besides, who would he leave his money to, he's getting on too, his health isn't

(20) good. His daughter? O, she's rolling in it, no fear of him leaving it to her, that husband of hers he hates. No, I'm going to put my foot down soon, see if I don't, I'm going to let her know that the bold

(25) Jimmy isn't the fine gentleman he pretends to be. Sure, how do I know what he takes her out for, if it isn't because she's the only person would listen to him and his eternal chat

(30) about New York? It's not the looks of her, he's not blind, maybe he thinks she has money too. Well, God knows, I can disabuse him of that idea. Either that or she's a miser, you should have seen her

(35) face when we were discussing the board and room and she never eats a decent meal, just snacks that would keep a bird

alive. O, when I think of it, all the prayers I've said and the novenas I've offered

(40) up that Jim would remember us over in America, since he got that money, and he was happy here, he wouldn't have forgotten us like this if she hadn't run after him.

Brian Moore, *The Lonely Passion of Judith Hearne*

1. Which word best describes the style of this passage?

   (1) formal
   (2) informal
   (3) academic
   (4) serious
   (5) complex

2. The author's choice of words conveys to readers that the narrator is

   (1) greedy
   (2) kind
   (3) shy
   (4) amused
   (5) generous

3. What is the effect of including only the narrator's words and not Bernie's?

   It shows that

   (1) Bernie is not really there
   (2) the narrator is a considerate conversationalist
   (3) Bernie agrees with the narrator
   (4) the narrator dominates the conversation
   (5) Bernie does not trust the narrator

4. Which of these methods of organization gives structure to the passage?

   (1) time order
   (2) cause and effect
   (3) compare and contrast
   (4) main idea and details
   (5) question and answer

Questions 5 through 8 refer to the following passage.

## IS THIS A FRIENDLY CHAT?

"Where you live? North Side, South Side, or West Side?" he probed further.

"North," the diner finally said.

"How far?"

(5)     "Too far," she said, cutting him short and touching the napkin to her lips.

"I live west myself—at Thirteenth and Tripp," he volunteered.

The diner sipped the rest of her Coke
(10)  but did not look in the bum's direction again.

He finished his pie quietly, drank the last of the coffee, and demanded a refill. Hattie rewarmed the coffee and asked
(15)  the female diner if everything was all right.

She nodded affirmatively.

"He ain't bothering you, is he, Doll?" Hattie asked.
(20)     The diner said no.

"You behave yourself," Hattie admonished the tramp with a raised finger. He leered at her and broke into a gravelly laugh.
(25)     "How much do I owe you?" he asked…

"Give me a dollar ninety-seven," Hattie replied, writing his total on the checkpad. She tore it off and placed it on the counter in front of him.
(30)     The derelict dug deep into his pocket and brought up a handful of change. Counting out the money to the penny, he slapped the coins onto the counter. Brushing away the loose tobacco from
(35)  among the nickels, dimes, pennies, and quarters, Hattie raked the money into her hand. When she went to the cash register to ring up the check, the beauty consultant blotted her lips again and
(40)  pushed her plate away. With her fork, she played with the french fries while she waited for Hattie to bring her check. Hattie returned with it, and the diner opened her purse, removed a ten from
(45)  her wallet, and laid it on the counter beside her plate. Then, as if she had thought the better of it, she picked up the bill and held it tightly in her hand until Hattie came for it.

Mark Allen Boone, "The Derelict"

5. Which of the following best describes the author's style?

(1) long, complex sentences
(2) narration rather than description
(3) formal, conventional language
(4) dialogue rather than narration
(5) detailed descriptions of actions

6. Which of the following is an example of nonstandard English?

(1) "Where you live? North Side, South Side, or West Side?"
(2) She nodded affirmatively.
(3) The diner said no.
(4) "You behave yourself," Hattie admonished the tramp with a raised finger.
(5) The derelict dug deep into his pocket and brought up a handful of change.

7. Line 18 is a good example of

(1) conventional style
(2) informal style
(3) humorous style
(4) standard English
(5) complex style

8. Which of these methods of organization gives structure to the passage?

(1) question and answer
(2) main idea and details
(3) cause and effect
(4) persuasive argument
(5) time order

**Answers and explanations start on page 116.**

[ **TIP**

Style is the way an author uses language. Think about what purpose or effect the author achieves by using language the way he or she does.

## Skill 17

# Interpret Tone of a Piece

Some questions on the GED Test will ask you to identify and interpret the **tone** of a piece of writing. Tone refers to the author's attitude toward the subject. In literature, tone is expressed through word choice, description, and punctuation.

To identify the tone, read the passage with expression. Try to sense the emotion behind the words and the attitude the emotion conveys.

**Read the passage. Choose the <u>one best answer</u> to the question.**

> When you are old and gray and full of sleep
> And nodding by the fire, take down this book,
> And slowly read, and dream of the soft look
> Your eyes had once, and of their shadows deep;
>
> How many loved your moments of glad grace,
> And loved your beauty with love false or true;
> But one man loved the pilgrim soul in you,
> And loved the sorrows of your changing face.
>
> And bending down beside the glowing bars,
> Murmur, a little sadly, how love fled
> And paced upon the mountains overhead,
> And hid his face amid a crowd of stars.

W. B. Yeats, "When You Are Old"

**QUESTION:** Which of the following best describes the tone of the poem?

(1) apologetic
(2) hopeful
(3) sad
(4) judgmental
(5) insistent

### EXPLANATIONS

**STEP 1** To answer this question, ask yourself:
- What is the poem about? <u>The speaker asks the reader to remember past loves.</u>
- What words and phrases are clues to the poet's attitude toward the subject he is writing about? <u>"old and gray," "had once," "loved," "a little sadly," "love fled"</u>

**STEP 2** Evaluate the answer choices. Which choice <u>best</u> expresses the tone?

(1) No. The poem's words and descriptions do not convey an apology.
(2) No. Hope is an attitude about the future. The poem is about the past.
(3) **Yes. Words and phrases such as *had once, loved, a little sadly,* and *love fled* emphasize the past and convey a feeling of sadness and nostalgia for what has been lost.**
(4) No. The poem's words do not suggest criticism.
(5) No. The poem does not insist on a single point of view.

**ANSWER: (3) sad**

# Practice the Skill

Try these examples. Choose the <u>one best answer</u> to each question. Then check your answers and read the explanations.

## WHAT KIND OF PERSON IS MR. GRADGRIND?

Thomas Gradgrind, sir. A man of realities. A man of facts and calculations. A man who proceeds upon the principle that two and two are four, and nothing over, and who is not to be talked into allowing for anything over. Thomas Gradgrind, sir—peremptorily Thomas—Thomas Gradgrind. With a rule and a pair of scales, and the multiplication table always in

(5)   his pocket, sir, ready to weigh and measure any parcel of human nature, and tell you exactly what it comes to. It is a mere question of figures, a case of simple arithmetic. You might hope to get some other nonsensical belief into the head of George Gradgrind, or Augustus Gradgrind, or John Gradgrind, or Joseph Gradgrind (all suppositions, all non-existent persons), but into the head of Thomas Gradgrind—no, sir!…

(10)   "Girl number twenty," said Mr. Gradgrind, squarely pointing with his square forefinger, "I don't know that girl. Who is that girl?"

"Sissy Jupe, sir," explained number twenty, blushing, standing up, and curtseying.

"Sissy is not a name," said Mr. Gradgrind. "Don't call yourself Sissy. Call yourself Cecilia."

(15)   "It's father as calls me Sissy, sir," …

"Then he has no business to do it," said Mr. Gradgrind. "Tell him he mustn't."

Charles Dickens, *Hard Times*

**1.** Which of the following best describes the tone of the passage?

(1)  disapproving
(2)  affectionate
(3)  amused
(4)  approving
(5)  fearful

**HINT** Which choice best describes the author's attitude toward his subject?

**2.** Which phrase from the passage is the best clue to its tone?

(1)  "two and two are four"
(2)  "a rule and a pair of scales"
(3)  "ready to weigh and measure any parcel of human nature"
(4)  "a case of simple arithmetic"
(5)  "blushing, standing up, and curtseying"

**HINT** Which phrase is a clue to the author's attitude toward his subject?

## Answers and Explanations

**1. (1) disapproving**
The author goes to the extreme in portraying Gradgrind as a no-nonsense, serious character. Such an over-the-top description reveals the author's own disapproval of someone who treats life so formally.

Options (2), (3), (4), and (5) are incorrect and not supported by the text.

**2. (3) "ready to weigh and measure any parcel of human nature"**
Option (3) is the correct answer. The author's reference to human nature as a "parcel" foreshadows what readers will learn later, when Mr. Gradgrind reveals his lack of concern for human feelings.

Options (1), (2), (4), and (5) are incorrect because they are not true keys to Gradgrind's nature.

# Interpret Tone of a Piece

**Directions: Choose the one best answer to each question.**

Questions 1 and 2 refer to the following passage.

## WHAT DOES THE LAW MEAN?

There is a state law on the books in Colorado that makes it illegal for a sheepherder to abandon his sheep without notice.

A good law, really, since herders are often left alone on isolated ranges with their entrusted band. The owner or boss usually checks on him once a week or so and brings him supplies. So, it would certainly create serious consequences were the sheep to be deserted and untended for any length of time.

But, to the uninformed—nonsheep people, that is—this law might seem a little unclear.

It could be interpreted to mean that the herder must notify his sheep before leaving them, to prevent emotional trauma, possibly, social breakdown, or obscure ovine behavioral disorders.

To comply with the law, he might line them up and give a sort of "going away" speech:

"My fellow ewes, lambs, and bucks. I have called you together to make an announcement. At approximately noon today, I intend to abandon you.

"It has not been an easy decision. I lay in my camp pondering the effect it would have on the herd. I agonized over leaving something that we've both worked so hard to establish. The caring and sincere bond we've formed that has made my job such a pleasure. The chuckles we've had and the times we've cried.

"I've asked a lot of you. At lambing, marking, and shearing, not to mention the time you all got footrot. Tough times. But you all gave it your best effort and survived. And, I think, y'all are better sheep for the experience.

"But people, just like sheep, grow and change. My needs are different, my horizons have expanded. I hope to enroll in a welding course at Community College and follow my star.

"I'm leaving you in good hands—or hooves, as it were. Paulita, I expect you to take over. You've been a strong example to the other ewes. Always first to water, first to new grass, and always willing to listen to the baa's and bleatings of others.

"Leadership is not an easy mantle to wear. And followers, you too, must blindly trust your leader and follow her like . . . well, like sheep."

Baxter Black, *Cactus Tracks and Cowboy Philosophy*

1. Which word best describes the tone of this passage?

   (1) serious
   (2) frustrated
   (3) humorous
   (4) demanding
   (5) concerned

2. Which sentence from the passage is the best clue to its overall tone?

   (1) "There is a state law on the books in Colorado that makes it illegal for a sheepherder to abandon his sheep without notice."
   (2) "But, to the uninformed—nonsheep people, that is—this law might seem a little unclear."
   (3) "It could be interpreted to mean that the herder must notify his sheep before leaving them, to prevent emotional trauma, possibly, social breakdown, or obscure ovine behavioral disorders."
   (4) "It has not been an easy decision."
   (5) "Leadership is not an easy mantle to wear."

Questions 3 through 5 refer to the following passage.

## IS BABBITT WELL DISCIPLINED?

Babbitt's preparations for leaving the office to its feeble self during the hour and a half of his lunch-period were somewhat less elaborate than the plans
(5) for a general European war.

He fretted to Miss McGoun, "What time you going to lunch? Well, make sure Miss Bannigan is in then. Explain to her that if Wiedenfeldt calls up, she's to tell
(10) him I'm already having the title traced. And oh, b' the way, remind me to-morrow to have Penniman trace it. Now if anybody comes in looking for a cheap house, remember we got to shove that
(15) Bangor Road place off onto somebody. If you need me, I'll be at the Athletic Club. And—uh—And—uh—I'll be back by two."

He dusted the cigar-ashes off his
(20) vest. He placed a difficult unanswered letter on the pile of unfinished work, that he might not fail to attend to it that afternoon. (For three noons, now, he had placed the same letter on
(25) the unfinished pile.) He scrawled on a sheet of yellow backing-paper the memorandum: "See abt apt h drs," which gave him an agreeable feeling of having already seen about the
(30) apartment-house doors.

He discovered he was smoking another cigar. He threw it away, protesting, "Darn it, I thought you'd quit this darn smoking!" He courageously
(35) returned the cigar-box to the correspondence-file, locked it up, hid the key in a more difficult place, and raged, "Ought to take care of myself. And need more exercise—walk to the club, every
(40) single noon—just what I'll do— every noon—cut out this motoring all the time."

The resolution made him feel exemplary. Immediately after it he decided that this noon it was too late
(45) to walk.

It took but little more time to start his car and edge it into the traffic than it would have taken to walk the three and a half blocks to the club.

Sinclair Lewis, *Babbitt*

3. Which word best describes the tone of this passage?

(1) respectful
(2) outraged
(3) sorrowful
(4) scornful
(5) tragic

4. Which sentence from the passage is the best clue to its overall tone?

(1) "Now if anybody comes in looking for a cheap house, remember we got to shove that Bangor Road place off onto somebody."
(2) "If you need me, I'll be at the Athletic Club."
(3) "He dusted the cigar ashes off his vest."
(4) "The resolution made him feel exemplary."
(5) "It took but little more time to start his car and edge it into the traffic than it would have taken to walk the three and a half blocks to the club."

5. The author's frequent use of dashes in this passage conveys that Babbitt is

(1) loud
(2) profane
(3) amusing
(4) thoughtful
(5) scatterbrained

> **TIP**
>
> When answering questions about tone, check your answer by rereading the passage and looking for words and punctuation marks that support your choice.

**Answers and explanations start on page 117.**

# Skill 18

# Determine Theme

Some questions on the GED Test will ask you to identify the **theme** of a passage. Theme refers to the central message, or point, of a passage. A theme may be directly stated; in other cases, a theme may be implied, or suggested. To find an implied theme, ask yourself, "What is this passage about? What point is made about the subject?" Because it is the author's message, a theme should always be a complete sentence.

**Read the passage. Choose the <u>one best answer</u> to the question.**

The hurt captain, lying against the water-jar in the bow, spoke always in a low voice and calmly, but he could never command a more ready and swiftly obedient crew than the motley three of the dingey. It was more than a mere recognition of what was best for the common safety. There was surely in
(5) it a quality that was personal and heartfelt. And after this devotion to the commander of the boat there was this comradeship that the correspondent, for instance, who had been taught to be cynical of men, knew even at the time was the best experience of his life. But no one said that it was so. No one mentioned it.

Stephen Crane, "The Open Boat"

**QUESTION:** What is the theme of the passage?

(1) Obedience is more important than friendship.
(2) Recognition does not always come to those who deserve it.
(3) Safety should always come first.
(4) Comradeship is both rewarding and practical.
(5) Cynicism can be dangerous.

**EXPLANATIONS**

**STEP 1**  To answer this question, ask yourself:
- What is the passage about? <u>Four men are in a boat. One, the leader, is hurt, and the men seem to be in some danger.</u>
- What is the central idea of the passage? <u>The men are cooperating out of a sense of mutual respect and comradeship.</u>

**STEP 2**  Evaluate the answer choices. Which choice <u>best</u> expresses the theme?

(1) No. The passage does not imply that obedience is more important than friendship.
(2) No. The passage does not say or imply this.
(3) No. The passage does not say that safety should always come first.
(4) **Yes. Lines 4–8 are all about comradeship. The narrator names comradeship as one reason why the men obeyed the captain and worked together well.**
(5) No. The passage does not say or imply that cynicism can be dangerous.

**ANSWER: (4) Comradeship is both rewarding and practical.**

Try these examples. Choose the <u>one best answer</u> to each question. Then check your answers and read the explanations.

## WHAT IS THE GHOST'S MESSAGE?

"Man of the worldly mind!" replied the Ghost, "do you believe in me or not?"

"I do," said Scrooge. "I must. But why do spirits walk the earth, and why do they come to me?"

"It is required of every man," the Ghost returned, "that the spirit within him should walk abroad among his fellowmen, and travel far and wide; and if that spirit goes not forth in life, it is condemned to do so after death. It is doomed to wander through the world—oh, woe is me!—and witness what it cannot share, but might have shared on earth, and turned to happiness!"

Again the spectre raised a cry, and shook its chain and wrung its shadowy hands.

"You are fettered," said Scrooge, trembling. "Tell me why?"

"I wear the chain I forged in life," replied the Ghost. "I made it link by link, and yard by yard; I girded it on of my own free will, and of my own free will I wore it."

Charles Dickens, *A Christmas Carol*

1. What is this passage about?

   (1) a ghost terrorizing an old man
   (2) a ghost warning an old man about what happens after death
   (3) a ghost telling jokes to an old man
   (4) an old man having a dream about a ghost
   (5) a ghost complaining about being tied up

   **HINT** Why is the ghost visiting Scrooge?

2. What is the theme of this passage?

   (1) Everyone experiences happiness after they die.
   (2) Everyone is doomed to wander the world after they die.
   (3) Your actions in life do not affect your fate after death.
   (4) Your actions in life influence your fate after death.
   (5) You should believe in ghosts and spirits.

   **HINT** What message does the ghost give Scrooge?

---

## Answers and Explanations

**1. (2) a ghost warning an old man about what happens after death**

Option (2) is correct. The ghost warns Scrooge that people who didn't enjoy life while living are doomed to wander the world after death.

Option (1) is incorrect; while scary, the ghost isn't terrorizing Scrooge—he's there to warn Scrooge to change his ways. Options (3) and (4) are incorrect; there's nothing regarding jokes or dreams in the passage. Option (5) is incorrect. While the ghost shows Scrooge his chain and explains why he has it, he does not complain about it.

**2. (4) Your actions in life influence your fate after death.**

Option (4) is correct. The ghost warns Scrooge that unfriendly people are doomed to wander the world after death, wearing a chain (a punishment for their mean life) and watching others enjoy life.

Options (1) and (2) are incorrect; according to the ghost, what happens after death is dependent upon how the person lived. Option (3) is incorrect; it is the opposite of the correct theme. Option (5) is incorrect; though the passage is about a ghost, it is a fictional story and does not represent the real world.

# Determine Theme

**Directions: Choose the one best answer to each question.**

Questions 1 through 3 refer to the following passage.

### WHAT IS THE BISHOP THINKING?

　　During those last weeks of the Bishop's life he thought very little about death; it was the Past he was leaving. The future would take care of itself. But he had an
(5)　intellectual curiosity about dying; about the changes that took place in a man's beliefs and scale of values. More and more life seemed to him an experience of the Ego, in no sense the Ego itself. This
(10)　conviction, he believed, was something apart from his religious life; it was an enlightenment that came to him as a man, a human creature. And he noticed that he judged conduct differently
(15)　now; his own and that of others. The mistakes of his life seemed unimportant; accidents that had occurred *en route*, like the shipwreck in Galveston harbour, or the runaway in which he was hurt
(20)　when he was first on his way to New Mexico in search of his Bishopric.
　　He observed also that there was no longer any perspective in his memories. He remembered his winters with his
(25)　cousins on the Mediterranean when he was a little boy, his student days in the Holy City, as clearly as he remembered the arrival of M. Molny and the building of his Cathedral. He was soon to have
(30)　done with calendared time, and it had already ceased to count for him. He sat in the middle of his own consciousness; none of his former states of mind were lost or outgrown. They were all within
(35)　reach of his hand, and all comprehensible.
　　Sometimes, when Magdalena or Bernard came in and asked him a question, it took him several seconds to bring himself back to the present. He

(40)　could see they thought his mind was failing; but it was only extraordinarily active in some other part of the great picture of his life—some part of which they knew nothing.

Willa Cather, *Death Comes for the Archbishop*

1. The passage is about a Bishop who

   (1) regrets his life
   (2) is afraid to die
   (3) must face death alone
   (4) sees his life in a new way
   (5) can no longer think clearly

2. What is the theme of the passage?

   (1) The living do not understand the dying.
   (2) People's religious beliefs may change when they are dying.
   (3) Dying people think about life in new and different ways than others.
   (4) It is a waste of time to live in the past.
   (5) Dying people should stay active and not dwell on death.

3. Which is the best clue to the theme?

   (1) "During those last weeks of the Bishop's life he thought very little about death...."
   (2) "But he had an intellectual curiosity about dying; about the changes that took place in a man's beliefs and scale of values."
   (3) "He remembered his winters with his cousins on the Mediterranean when he was a little boy, his students days in the Holy City, as clearly as he remembered the arrival of M. Molny and the building of his Cathedral."
   (4) "Sometimes, ... it took him several seconds to bring himself back to the present."
   (5) "He could see they thought his mind was failing...."

Questions 4 through 6 refer to the following poem.

## HOW SHOULD YOU LIVE?

If you can keep your head when all about you
Are losing theirs and blaming it on you;
If you can trust yourself when all men doubt
   you,
But make allowance for their doubting too;
If you can wait and not be tired by waiting,
Or, being lied about, don't deal in lies,
Or, being hated, don't give way to hating,
And yet don't look too good, nor talk too wise;

If you can dream—and not make dreams your
   master;
If you can think—and not make thoughts your
   aim;
If you can meet with triumph and disaster
And treat those two impostors just the same;
If you can bear to hear the truth you've spoken
Twisted by knaves to make a trap for fools,
Or watch the things you gave your life to
   broken,
And stoop and build 'em up with wornout
   tools;

If you can make one heap of all your winnings
And risk it on one turn of pitch-and-toss,
And lose, and start again at your beginnings
And never breathe a word about your loss;
If you can force your heart and nerve and
   sinew
To serve your turn long after they are gone,
And so hold on when there is nothing in you
Except the Will which says to them: "Hold on";

If you can talk with crowds and keep your
   virtue,
Or walk with kings—nor lose the common
   touch;

If neither foes nor loving friends can hurt you;
If all men count with you, but none too much;
If you can fill the unforgiving minute
With sixty seconds' worth of distance run—
Yours is the Earth and everything that's in it,
And—which is more—you'll be a Man, my son!

          Rudyard Kipling, "If—"

4. What is this poem about?

  (1) how to become rich
  (2) how children should behave
  (3) how to make friends with kings
  (4) how to avoid disasters completely
  (5) how a mature person should behave

5. What is the theme of this poem?

  (1) You should be willing to risk everything.
  (2) You should always stand up for yourself.
  (3) Physical stamina is more important than
      mental stamina.
  (4) Acting with maturity and dignity gives
      you power.
  (5) Only men should be mature and
      dignified.

6. Which of the following lines best supports
   the theme?

  (1) "If you can meet with triumph and
      disaster"
  (2) "Are losing theirs and blaming it on you;"
  (3) "Or, being hated, don't give way to
      hating,"
  (4) "Twisted by knaves to make a trap for
      fools,"
  (5) "And risk it on one turn of pitch-and-
      toss,"

> ## TIP
>
> When you look for the theme of a
> passage, ask yourself, "Why did this
> author choose this situation? These
> characters? This conflict? What
> central message is the author trying
> to communicate?"

**Answers and explanations start on page 117.**

# Skill 19

# Compare and Contrast

For some items on the GED Test, you will be asked to **compare and contrast** two characters or two things. When you compare things, you identify ways they are similar. When you contrast things, you tell how they are different. You may notice their different sizes, shapes, qualities, or characteristics.

**Read the passage. Choose the <u>one best answer</u> to the question.**

In a desire to protect the environment, many people have turned to electric lawnmowers. All models produce a disconcerting hum when turned on, especially if you're used to the racket of a gasoline engine. The primary difference among electric mowers is the power source. Rechargeable mowers have no cord and are powered by an on-board battery that must be recharged before each use. Corded models have a power cord that attaches to an extension cord that you plug into an exterior outlet. Rechargeables can go anywhere, and you don't have to worry about running over a cord or pulling one around as you navigate. They are generally less powerful than corded models, and when the battery begins to drain, performance suffers quickly. You may have to go through a couple of charging cycles if your lawn is large. Corded models run as long as you like, but you are limited by the length of your extension cord and your patience in fooling with it. Neither is as effective at cutting grass as the old-fashioned piston engine, but neither ever sends you to a gas pump and both are better for the air and the quiet of your neighborhood.

**QUESTION:** Which of the following is a similarity between the two types of electric lawnmowers?

(1) length of cord
(2) rechargeable battery
(3) they use no gasoline
(4) piston engine
(5) requires exterior outlet

## EXPLANATIONS

**STEP 1**

To answer this question, ask yourself:
- What is this passage about? <u>two types of electric lawnmowers</u>
- How are the two types of electric lawnmowers the same? <u>They both hum, they don't use gasoline, and they are quieter than gas models.</u>

**STEP 2**

Evaluate the answer choices. Which item is the <u>best</u> choice?

(1) No. Only corded models have cords.
(2) No. Only rechargeable models have rechargeable batteries.
(3) **Yes. The benefit of an electric lawnmower is that it uses no gasoline.**
(4) No. Electric lawnmowers do not have piston engines.
(5) No. Only the corded models require an outlet.

**ANSWER: (3) they use no gasoline**

# Practice the Skill

Try these examples. Choose the one best answer to each question. Then check your answers and read the explanations.

## WHO ARE THESE MEN?

He had his kids lined up just so, as you would expect, and his shoes were shined beyond any natural gleam. He didn't have to wear his uniform, which was a little tight, I thought, but it occurred to me it could be the best suit he had, or maybe he just wanted to go all-out. I had to admit he looked pretty crisp despite his softening shape, and I felt an odd kind of respect

(5) for what I had long disdained. My jacket and shoes were names he'd never heard and my gym-flogged silhouette was trim, but I felt a little drab, for I was neither wearing twenty years of medals nor hardened by decades of obedience. Still, Mr. Military was pretty rattled. In the anteroom, he looked at me expectantly, eagerly somehow, though grimly, and we clasped hands awkwardly. His hair was sticking up, kind of surprising as he wore it so short. I

(10) reached up and tucked his tie in beside his neck and rolled his collar down. Had he not looked in the mirror? Just before I left the hotel I had glanced, and there still, despite a respectable haircut and the rounding jowls of the years, was yet the dim trace of the protestor, the sandal-wearing hippie, the McGovern campaign employee, the relentless activist and agitator, the insolent brother who would not shut up, and here, now, was his successor

(15) gently patting into place the black standard-issue tie of his chief antagonist and target. We went into the casket room.

Edward Coulon, "Patriots"

**1. What do the men share?**

(1) a military past
(2) a fondness for suits
(3) their family history
(4) family resemblance
(5) a calm demeanor

**HINT** What details does the passage provide about each person?

**2. How is the narrator different from his brother?**

(1) He has different political views.
(2) He has aged and gotten soft.
(3) He wears his hair very short.
(4) He doesn't have children.
(5) He wore his best suit.

**HINT** Which details describe the narrator? Which are about the brother?

---

## Answers and Explanations

**1. (3) their family history**
Option (3) correctly names what the two men share. They are brothers (line 14).

Option (1) is not correct because only one brother is noted to have a military past. Option (2) is not correct because one brother wears a uniform, which is different from his brother's "jacket." Option (4) is incorrect because no information is given about family resemblance. Option (5) contradicts the statement that "Mr. Military was pretty rattled."

**2. (1) He has different political views.**
Option (1) is supported by lines 13 and 14, where the narrator describes views that had differed and doubtless annoyed his brother, the soldier.

Option (2) is not correct because the narrator has a trim, "gym-flogged silhouette." Option (3) is not correct because the narrator says he has a "respectable haircut," which does not necessarily mean "very short." Option (4) is not correct because there is no indication of whether the narrator has children. Option (5) is not supported in the passage.

# Compare and Contrast

**Directions: Choose the <u>one best answer</u> to each question.**

<u>Questions 1 through 4</u> refer to the following passage.

### HOW ARE THESE MEN ALIKE?

Bertie was a barrister and a man of letters, a Scotchman of the intellectual type, quick, ironical, sentimental, and on his knees before the woman he adored
(5) but did not want to marry. Maurice Pervin was different. He came of a good old country family—the Grange was not a very great distance from Oxford. He was passionate, sensitive, perhaps
(10) oversensitive, wincing—a big fellow with heavy limbs and a forehead that flushed painfully. For his mind was slow, as if drugged by the strong provincial blood that beat in his veins. He was very
(15) sensitive to his own mental slowness, his feelings being quick and acute. So that he was just the opposite to Bertie, whose mind was much quicker than his emotions, which were not so very fine.
(20) From the first the two men did not like each other. Isabel felt that they ought to get on together. But they did not. She felt that if only each could have the clue to the other there would be such a rare
(25) understanding between them. It did not come off, however. Bertie adopted a slightly ironical attitude, very offensive to Maurice, who returned the Scotch irony with English resentment, a resentment
(30) which deepened sometimes into stupid hatred.
This was a little puzzling to Isabel. However, she accepted it in the course of things. Men were made freakish and
(35) unreasonable. Therefore, when Maurice was going out to France for the second time, she felt that, for her husband's sake, she must discontinue her friendship with Bertie. She wrote to the barrister

(40) to this effect. Bertram Reid simply replied that in this, as in all other matters, he must obey her wishes, if these were indeed her wishes.

D.H. Lawrence, "The Blind Man"

1. How does Bertie differ from Maurice?
   (1) Bertie is a military man.
   (2) Bertie is English.
   (3) Bertie thinks quickly.
   (4) Bertie is sensitive to others' feelings.
   (5) Bertie is not very sentimental.

2. What do the two men have in common?
   (1) cultural heritage
   (2) ancestors
   (3) physical build
   (4) occupations
   (5) a fondness for Isabel

3. Which of the following is a statement about Maurice Pervin?
   (1) His intellect drives his every action.
   (2) It is always hard to tell what he is feeling.
   (3) He is more emotional than intellectual.
   (4) He is domineering of his wife.
   (5) He gets along easily with everyone.

4. Why is it unsurprising that Bertie seems to comply with Isabel's wish to discontinue their friendship?
   (1) He only pretended to be her friend for the sake of his business.
   (2) He does not wish to offend Isabel, yet he hints that the relationship must end only "if these were indeed her wishes."
   (3) He so disliked Maurice that he was only too glad to discontinue the friendship.
   (4) He was extremely sensitive and was empathetic to Isabel's concerns with Maurice leaving for France.
   (5) Because he was slow-witted, he didn't fully understand that Isabel was asking to discontinue the relationship.

Questions 5 through 10 refer to the following passage.

## LIKE OR UNLIKE?

Shall I compare thee to a summer's day?
Thou art more lovely and more temperate.
Rough winds do shake the darling buds
    of May,
(5)  and summer's lease hath all too short
    a date.
Sometime too hot the eye of heaven
    shines,
And often is his gold complexion dimmed;
(10)  And every fair from fair sometime
    declines,
By chance, or nature's changing course,
    untrimmed:
But thy eternal summer shall not fade
(15)  Nor lose possession of that fair thou
    ow'st,
Nor shall Death brag thou wand'rest in
    his shade
When in eternal lines to time thou grow'st.
(20)    So long as men can breathe or eyes
    can see,
    So long lives this, and this gives life to
    thee.

William Shakespeare, "Sonnet 18"

5. What two things are being considered in this sonnet?

(1) the present and the past
(2) lovely weather and rough weather
(3) a loved one and a summer day
(4) sunshine and shadow
(5) summer and autumn

6. Line 2, "Thou art more lovely and more temperate," could be restated as:

(1) "You are beautiful but hot-tempered."
(2) "You are like a nice summer day."
(3) "You are unpredictable in your nature."
(4) "You are prettier than a summer day."
(5) "You are too cool and calm for me."

7. Lines 3–4, "Rough winds do shake the darling buds of May," show that

(1) a person's emotions vary
(2) summer is not always so pleasant
(3) trouble comes to every relationship
(4) it is not yet summer
(5) beauty will always endure

8. What contrast do lines 7–14 make?

(1) Both summer and his love are golden.
(2) Both summer and his love are fair.
(3) His love sometimes gets an angry look in her eye.
(4) His love will grow old and die, but summer's beauty will last forever.
(5) Summer beauty fades, but his love's beauty will live forever.

9. Line 14, "But thy eternal summer shall not fade," means:

(1) You will never die.
(2) Seasons change but we need not.
(3) I will never forget you as long as I live.
(4) Your beauty will outlast every summer.
(5) Summer returns every year.

10. What does the poem finally contrast?

(1) the short-lived beauty of love to the long-lived nature of friendship
(2) the brief beauty of life to the ongoing life of poetry
(3) the endurance of love to the changeableness of weather
(4) the image of summer to the inevitable return of autumn
(5) the short length of a poem to the enduring quality of true love

> **TIP**
>
> The reason to make a comparison or contrast is to discover or learn something by examining the items closely. For both comparison and contrast, think about the point that is made or what you learn from the technique.

**Answers and explanations start on page 118.**

Synthesis

# Integrate Outside Information

For some items on the GED Test, you will be asked **integrate outside information**. To integrate is to put two things or thoughts together. When you integrate outside information, you add a piece of knowledge or information from one source to another source in order to look at the information in another way or to answer an entirely new question. To integrate information, you must understand main ideas, details, and implications in order to apply ideas, make inferences, and draw conclusions.

**Read the passage. Choose the one best answer to the question.**

## WHAT ARE THE CONSEQUENCES OF DEBT?

Americans are caught up in a spending frenzy. There were an estimated 176 million credit card holders in 2008; they held 1.9 billion credit cards—about nine cards per credit card holder. From 2001 to 2006, Citicorp used the slogan "Live Richly" to encourage Americans to increase spending by taking out loans.

According to the Federal Reserve, total consumer debt topped out at $2.5 trillion in 2007. That's roughly $8,200 for every man, woman, and child in the country. Perhaps more unbelievable is that this debt consists mainly of credit card, vehicle, and student loan debt; it does not include home loans.

**QUESTION:** The 2007 mortgage crisis saw record numbers of people foreclosing on their homes, unable to pay their mortgage. This is probably because

  (1) home loan rates are typically very affordable
  (2) banks prefer to make home loans to people who have lots of debt
  (3) Americans do not have the incomes they once had
  (4) more income is going to payments on other types of debt
  (5) most Americans do not work as hard as they once did

### EXPLANATIONS

**STEP 1** To answer this question, ask yourself:
  • What is this passage about? <u>historically high levels of American debt</u>
  • What does the question ask me to do? <u>Integrate information about American consumer debt with the fact that record numbers of people have been unable to pay their mortgage.</u>

**STEP 2** Evaluate the answer choices. Which item is the <u>best</u> choice?

  (1) No. This would make home ownership easier, not more difficult.
  (2) No. Banks prefer to make home loans to people who have low debt.
  (3) No. Total income is not as important as how the money is spent.
  (4) **Yes. If more income is going to other debts, then less is available for paying a mortgage.**
  (5) No. Working hard is not related to making good financial choices.

**ANSWER: (4) more income is going to payments on other types of debt**

# Practice the Skill

Try these examples. Choose the **one best answer** to each question. Then check your answers and read the explanations.

## HOW HAVE FASHIONS CHANGED?

Miss Brill put up her hand and touched her fur. Dear little thing! It was nice to feel it again. She had taken it out of its box that afternoon, shaken out the moth powder, given it a good brush, and rubbed the life back into the dim little eyes. "What has been happening to me?" said the sad little eyes. Oh, how sweet it was to see them snap at her again from the red

(5)  eiderdown!...But the nose, which was of some black composition, wasn't at all firm. It must have had a knock, somehow. Never mind—a little dab of black sealing wax when the time came—when it was absolutely necessary...Little rogue! Yes, she really felt like that about it. Little rogue biting its tail just by her left ear. She could have taken it off and laid it on her lap and stroked it. She felt a tingling in her hands and arms, but that came from walking, she

(10) supposed. And when she breathed, something light and sad—no, not sad exactly—something gentle seemed to move in her bosom.

Katherine Mansfield, "Miss Brill"

1. Which is the <u>best</u> description of the fur?

   (1) It is a jacket rarely worn over the years.
   (2) It is a wrap that includes the head and tail of the animal.
   (3) It is a full-length coat of rare white mink.
   (4) It was a gift and had been in storage for the summer.
   (5) It is an imported fur.

   **HINT** What details does the passage provide about the fur?

2. Since its height in the 1920s, the market for furs has dropped dramatically. This is probably because

   (1) new materials are less expensive and more appealing
   (2) most people use nothing made from animals anymore
   (3) people no longer buy things that are purely luxury items
   (4) it is not possible to raise enough animals for fur to meet demand
   (5) most governments no longer allow fur to be sold

   **HINT** What factors might affect the use of furs for clothing?

---

## Answers and Explanations

**1. (2) It is a wrap that includes the head and tail of the animal.**

Option (2) best describes Miss Brill's small wrap because it has eyes (line 3), a nose (line 5), and a tail (line 8).

Option (1) is not correct because it is a fur, not a jacket, and it can be inferred that she has worn it often over the years. Option (3) is not correct because nothing in the passage identifies the species of animal. Option (4) is incorrect because although the fur has been in storage, no information is given about the time of year or where she got it. Option (5) is incorrect because there is no information about the fur's source.

**2. (1) new materials are less expensive and more appealing**

Option (1) is the best choice. There are many materials available today that were not around in the 1920s, and synthetic furs are now more popular than real furs.

Option (2) is incorrect because many people continue to use animal products, such as leather and for food. Option (3) is not correct; people still buy many luxury items. Option (4) is incorrect; supply usually follows demand. Option (5) is incorrect; fur products are still widely available.

# Integrate Outside Information

**Directions: Choose the one best answer to each question.**

Questions 1 through 4 refer to the following passage.

## WHAT HAPPENED TO THE KINGDOM?

### OZYMANDIAS

I met a traveler from an antique land.
Who said: Two vast and trunkless legs
    of stone
Stand in the desert...Near them, on
(5)     the sand
Half sunk, a shattered visage lies,
    whose frown,
And wrinkled lip, and sneer of cold
    command,
(10)  Tell that its sculptor well those passions
    read
Which yet survive, stamped on these
    lifeless things,
The head that mocked them, and the
(15)    heart that fed:
And on the pedestal these words appear:
"My name is Ozymandias, king of kings:
Look on my works, ye Mighty, and
    despair!"
(20)  Nothing beside remains. Round the
    decay
Of that colossal wreck, boundless
    and bare
The lone and level sands stretch far away.

Percy Bysshe Shelley, "Ozymandias"

1. What happened to the great ruler?

    (1) He was defeated by another.
    (2) He grew old and died.
    (3) He fell victim to disease.
    (4) He was assassinated by his son.
    (5) not enough information

2. Many cultures have considered their rulers to be divine, or approved by divinity. This is probably a result of

    (1) great monuments dedicated to the rulers
    (2) stories told to glorify the kings
    (3) the ruler's military skill and power
    (4) the illiteracy of most ancient cultures
    (5) the comparative simplicity of ancient religions

3. What might the shattered statue symbolize?

    (1) the power of a competing kingdom
    (2) the wealth of ancient societies today
    (3) the superior cultures of ancient peoples
    (4) the impermanence of human works
    (5) the timelessness of ancient art

4. Many societies have risen and fallen over the centuries. Often we know little or nothing about them because

    (1) they were not truly as powerful as their legends claim
    (2) their primitive religions were secretive and confusing
    (3) their cities were destroyed by fires
    (4) their records and artifacts have disappeared
    (5) they were not usually worth detailed study

> **TIP**
>
> To integrate information, add what you learn to a circumstance, and then try to predict or draw a conclusion. Ask yourself "How does the new information change what I know? What might happen as a result?"

Questions 5 through 7 refer to the following passage.

## WHO IS PURUN DASS?

But as Purun Dass grew up he realized that the ancient order of things was changing, and that if anyone wished to get on in the world he must stand well with the English, and imitate all that the English believed to be good. At the same time a native official must keep his master's favour. This was a difficult game, but the quiet, close-mouthed young Brahmin, helped by a good English education at a Bombay university, played it coolly, and rose, step by step, to be Prime Minister of the kingdom. That is to say, he held more real power than his master, the Maharajah.

When the old king—who was suspicious of the English, their railways and telegraphs—died, Purun Dass stood high with his young successor, who had been tutored by an Englishman; and between them, though he always took care that his master should have the credit, they established schools for little girls, made roads, and started State dispensaries and shows of agricultural implements, and published a yearly blue-book on the "Moral and Material Progress of the State," and the Foreign Office and the Government of India were delighted. Very few native States take up English progress without reservations, for they will not believe, as Purun Dass showed he did, that what is good for the Englishman must be twice as good for the Asiatic. The Prime Minister became the honoured friend of Viceroys and Governors, and Lieutenant-Governors, and medical missionaries, and common missionaries, and hard riding English officers who came to shoot in the State preserves, as well as whole hosts of tourists who travelled up and down India in cold weather, showing how things ought to be managed. In his spare time he would endow scholarships for the study of medicine and manufacturers on strictly English lines, and write letters to the *Pioneer*, the greatest Indian daily paper, explaining his master's aims and objects.

Rudyard Kipling, "The Miracle of Purun Bhagat"

5. Purun Dass's efforts seem to be directed at

(1) working to achieve independence for the Indian people
(2) improving India in a way that is acceptable to the British
(3) defending and preserving the Indian way of life
(4) blocking British efforts to change India
(5) making the Maharajah look bad in front of the British

6. At the time this story was written, India was a part of the British Empire. England ruled the country, and Indians governed in local states. This fact probably accounts for

(1) Purun Dass's deep resentment of the British
(2) Purun Dass's disloyalty to his own people
(3) Purun Dass's attempt to balance his role between the British and the Indians
(4) Purun Dass's rapid rise to a position of power in the Indian government
(5) Purun Dass's inability to make changes in the nature of Indian life

7. In 1947, India gained complete independence from Great Britain. How would you expect circumstances to have changed since then?

(1) Few significant changes would have taken place.
(2) All traces of British influence would have disappeared.
(3) Indian culture and customs would have come to prevail in the country.
(4) England would continue to advise India on its actions.
(5) England and India would become enemies.

**Answers and explanations start on page 119.**

# GED

Tests of
General Educational
Development

# Language Arts, Reading
Official GED Practice Test

GED Testing Service
American Council on Education

**LANGUAGE ARTS, READING**

Tests of General Educational Development

**Directions**

The Language Arts, Reading Test consists of excerpts from fiction and nonfiction. Each excerpt is followed by multiple-choice questions about the reading material.

Read each excerpt first and then answer the questions following it. Refer back to the reading material as often as necessary in answering the questions.

Each excerpt is preceded by a "purpose question." The purpose question gives a reason for reading the material. Use these purpose questions to help focus your reading. You are not required to answer these purpose questions. They are given only to help you concentrate on the ideas presented in the reading material.

You will have 33 minutes to answer the 20 questions in this booklet. Work carefully, but do not spend too much time on any one question. Be sure you answer every question.

Do not mark in this test booklet. Record your answers on the separate answer sheet provided. Be sure that all requested information is properly recorded on the answer sheet.

To record your answers, fill in the numbered circle on the answer sheet that corresponds to the answer you select for each question in the test booklet.

---

FOR EXAMPLE:

It was Susan's dream machine. The metallic blue paint gleamed, and the sporty wheels were highly polished. Under the hood, the engine was no less carefully cleaned. Inside, flashy lights illuminated the instruments on the dashboard, and the seats were covered by rich leather upholstery.

The subject ("It") of this excerpt is most likely

(1)  an airplane
(2)  a stereo system
(3)  an automobile
(4)  a boat
(5)  a motorcycle

(On Answer Sheet)
① ② ● ④ ⑤

The correct answer is "an automobile"; therefore, answer space 3 would be marked on the answer sheet.

---

Do not rest the point of your pencil on the answer sheet while you are considering your answer. Make no stray or unnecessary marks. If you change an answer, erase your first mark completely. Mark only <u>one</u> answer space for each question; multiple answers will be scored as incorrect. Do not fold or crease your answer sheet. All test materials must be returned to the test administrator.

**DO NOT BEGIN TAKING THIS TEST UNTIL TOLD TO DO SO**

Component: 9993949116
Kit: **ISBN 0-7398-5433-X**

4                                    **Reading**

<u>Directions</u>: Choose the <u>one best answer</u> to each question.

<u>Questions 1 through 6</u> refer to the following poem.

### HOW DOES THE SPEAKER RELATE TO THE LIFE OF A CAGED BIRD?

Sympathy

I know what the caged bird feels, alas!
When the sun is bright on the upland slopes;
When the wind stirs through the springing grass,
And the river flows like a stream of glass;
(5)   When the first bird sings and the first bud opes [opens],
And the faint perfume from its chalice steals—
I know what the caged bird feels!

I know why the caged bird beats his wing
Till its blood is red on the cruel bars;
(10)   For he must fly back to his perch and cling
When he fain would be on the bough a-swing;
And a pain still throbs in the old, old scars
And they pulse again with a keener sting—
I know why he beats his wing!

(15)   I know why the caged bird sings, ah, me,
When his wing is bruised and his bosom sore,—
When he beats his bars and he would be free;
It is not a carol of joy or glee,
But a prayer that he sends from the heart's deep core,
(20)   But a plea, that upward to Heaven he flings—
I know why the caged bird sings!

Paul Laurence Dunbar, "Sympathy," 1899.

**GO ON TO THE NEXT PAGE**

1. In lines 1–6, the speaker describes the world outside the bird's cage. From the caged bird's point of view, what does the outside world represent?

   (1) spring
   (2) freedom
   (3) vacation
   (4) love
   (5) youth

2. What feeling is the speaker attributing to the caged bird's song in lines 19–20: "But a prayer that he sends from the heart's deep core, / But a plea, that upward to Heaven he flings"?

   (1) anger
   (2) playfulness
   (3) longing
   (4) relaxation
   (5) betrayal

3. Notice that most of the words of the first line of each stanza are repeated at the end of that stanza. What effect does this repetition have on the speaker's message?

   The repetition

   (1) reinforces the speaker's message
   (2) mocks the message of the first line
   (3) makes other rhyming unnecessary
   (4) restates the title
   (5) makes interpreting the ideas more difficult

4. From what you know of the speaker in the poem, what feelings might he or she have toward someone in slavery?

   (1) understanding
   (2) indifference
   (3) fondness
   (4) embarrassment
   (5) hatred

5. Which among the following is the most likely occasion for someone to sing a song similar to the song of the bird?

   (1) a vacation in the mountains
   (2) a young children's sing-along
   (3) a birthday celebration
   (4) a peaceful protest
   (5) a nighttime lullaby

6. Maya Angelou, an African American writer, titled her autobiography *I Know Why the Caged Bird Sings*. What does her use of the line from the poem "Sympathy" in her title suggest about the message of her book?

   Angelou's book is about

   (1) success after extensive failure
   (2) maltreatment of caged animals
   (3) the enjoyment of springtime
   (4) capturing and charging criminals
   (5) understanding the suffering of others

**GO ON TO THE NEXT PAGE**

6                                            **Reading**

<u>Questions 7 through 12</u> refer to the following excerpt.

## WHAT IS THE RELATIONSHIP BETWEEN JIM AND ANTONIA?

She turned her bright, believing eyes to me, and the tears came up in them slowly, "How can it be like that, when you know so many people, and when
(5) I've disappointed you so? Ain't it wonderful, Jim, how much people can mean to each other? I'm so glad we had each other when we were little. I can't wait till my little girl's old enough
(10) to tell her about all the things we used to do. You'll always remember me when you think about old times, won't you? And I guess everybody thinks about old times, even the happiest people."

(15) As we walked homeward across the fields, the sun dropped and lay like a great golden globe in the low west. While it hung there, the moon rose in the east, as big as a cart-wheel, pale
(20) silver and streaked with rose colour, thin as a bubble or a ghost-moon. For five perhaps ten minutes, the two luminaries confronted each other across the level land, resting on opposite edges of the
(25) world.

In that singular light every little tree and shock of wheat, every sunflower stalk and clump of snow-on-the-mountain, drew itself up high and
(30) pointed; the very clods and furrows in the fields seemed to stand up sharply. I felt the old pull of the earth, the solemn magic that comes out of those fields at nightfall. I wished I could be a little boy
(35) again, and that my way could end there.

We reached the edge of the field, where our ways parted. I took her hands and held them against my breast, feeling once more how strong and warm
(40) and good they were, those brown hands, and remembering how many kind things they had done for me. I held them now a long while, over my heart. About us it was growing darker and
(45) darker, and I had to look hard to see her face, which I meant always to carry with me; the closest, realest face, under all the shadows of women's faces, at the very bottom of my memory.

(50) "I'll come back," I said earnestly, through the soft, intrusive darkness.

"Perhaps you will"—I felt rather than saw her smile. "But even if you don't, you're here, like my father. So I won't
(55) be lonesome."

As I went back alone over that familiar road, I could almost believe that a boy and girl ran along beside me, as our shadows used to do, laughing and
(60) whispering to each other in the grass.

Willa Cather, *My Antonia*, 1918.

**GO ON TO THE NEXT PAGE**

7. When Antonia says, "I guess everybody thinks about old times, even the happiest people" (lines 13–14), what is she suggesting about Jim?

   Jim is

   (1) happy in his new life but also happy to remember his childhood with her
   (2) so unhappy in his new life that he often thinks of her
   (3) happy enough in his new life that he no longer needs her
   (4) so unhappy in his new life that he can't bear his happy memories of her
   (5) happiest when he is daydreaming about his past with her

8. On the basis of Antonia's character as revealed in this excerpt, how would she most likely act toward Jim if he returned in the future?

   She would probably

   (1) accuse him of ignoring her
   (2) demand that he leave again immediately
   (3) welcome him with friendship
   (4) cling to him passionately
   (5) insist that he stay with her forever

9. On the basis of Jim's character as revealed in this excerpt, what relationship is he likely to have with Antonia in the future?

   He will

   (1) write to her often
   (2) stay with her
   (3) forget his friendship with her
   (4) think of her often
   (5) resent her

10. The boy and girl who run along beside Jim as he leaves are which of the following?

    (1) Antonia's children
    (2) Jim and Antonia's children
    (3) Jim's memories of himself and Antonia as children
    (4) children who now live on the farm
    (5) Jim's spirit as he walks away

11. When Antonia tells Jim that he is here, like her father, she is implying which of the following?

    (1) Although her father is dead, he still runs her life.
    (2) Because she lives with her father, she does not need Jim's company.
    (3) Since her father abandoned her, she has gotten used to loneliness.
    (4) Because of her children, Antonia needs neither the memory of Jim or her father.
    (5) Because she has memories of her father and Jim, she does not feel alone.

12. In an earlier part of this story, the reader learns that Jim moved away and has become a lawyer. Based on this information and the passage, what does Jim understand about his relationship with Antonia?

    (1) He will have to stay with Antonia forever.
    (2) He can never come back because she is married and does not wish to see him again.
    (3) He should never have come because they now have nothing in common.
    (4) He and Antonia will always treasure their wonderful shared memories of childhood.
    (5) His early years are of no importance to him now.

**GO ON TO THE NEXT PAGE**

8                                                        Reading

Questions 13 through 16 refer to the following business document.

# HOW MUST EMPLOYEES BEHAVE?

## Strathmore College Employee Handbook

### Employee Performance: Discipline and Dismissal

The College recognizes the importance of establishing and maintaining good working relationships with its personnel.  However, problems of job performance and misconduct may arise and will be addressed with disciplinary actions.  These actions include a process of verbal warnings, written warnings, and dismissal, when a situation warrants.

(5)   **Just Cause**
The College will not normally discipline or dismiss an employee without just cause.  Just cause includes but is not limited to

a.   failure to perform one's duties satisfactorily;

b.   insubordination, which is defined as willful failure to follow a legitimate order;

(10)   c.   consumption of intoxicants or use, possession, or sale of legally prohibited or controlled substances on College property, or attendance at work under the influence of intoxicants or legally prohibited controlled substances;

d.   absence from work without authorization or appropriate excuse, or habitual tardiness;

e.   excessive absenteeism, which is defined as repeated absences from work that are
(15)   not included in an approved formal leave of absence;

f.   willful falsification or alteration of a College record (including employment applications or resumés);

g.   conviction of a felony or other crime, the nature of which is such that continued employment may be disruptive to College operations;

(20)   h.   presenting a possible or potential danger to the safety of other employees, the public, or College property;

i.   unlawful sexual harassment as defined by Federal and/or State law; and

j.   any other action detrimental to the College while on College property or while engaged in College work.

**GO ON TO THE NEXT PAGE**

13. According to the document, which one of the following is a "just cause" (lines 6–24)?

    (1) excused absences from work
    (2) following legitimate orders
    (3) making a mistake on a job application
    (4) getting a parking ticket
    (5) sexual harassment

14. What is the main purpose of the College's just cause policy?

    (1) to build employee morale at the College
    (2) to prevent harassment cases from going to court
    (3) to protect the College from hiring incompetent employees
    (4) to help employees conceal misconduct from the College
    (5) to make clear to employees the rules for discipline and dismissal

15. Which of the following would be an example of "willful falsification or alteration of a College record" (line 16)?

    (1) copying a page out of the College catalog
    (2) correcting an error in a student's record
    (3) forgetting to change your address on your record after you have moved
    (4) giving an incorrect date of graduation in your employment history
    (5) leaving the file room door unlocked overnight

16. If the College wanted to discipline an employee for a minor problem, what would be the first step?

    (1) warning in writing
    (2) excessive absenteeism
    (3) verbal warning
    (4) dismissal
    (5) loss of pay

**GO ON TO THE NEXT PAGE**

10                              Reading

Questions 17 through 20 refer to the following excerpt from a play.

### DOES CORIE'S MOTHER LIKE THIS APARTMENT?

[Corie's mother, Mrs. Banks, staggers in the door, bouncing off it and coming to rest paralyzed against the railing. While she is regaining her breath, Corie brings
(5) her a glass of water and leads her to a suitcase so that she can sit.]

**MOTHER:** I really had no intention of coming up, but I had a luncheon in Westchester and I thought, since it's
(10) on my way home, I might as well drop in for a few minutes. . . .

**CORIE:** On your way to New Jersey?

**MOTHER:** Yes, I came over the Whitestone Bridge and down the
(15) Major Deegan Highway and now I'll cut across town and onto the Henry Hudson Parkway and up to the George Washington Bridge. It's no extra trouble.

(20) [Corie tells her they want her to come visit them on Friday after the furniture is there. Mrs. Banks makes light of the lack of furniture and stands up with the intention of praising the apartment.
(25) However, its bleakness stops her cold and all she can do is force out a lie through gritted teeth.]

**MOTHER:** (Stunned) Oh, Corie . . . it's . . . beautiful.

(30) **CORIE:** You hate it. . . .

**MOTHER:** (Moves up toward windows) No, no. . . . It's a charming apartment. (Trips over platform) I love it.

(35) **CORIE:** (Rushes to her) You can't really tell like this.

**MOTHER:** I'm crazy about it. I love it. . . .

**CORIE:** Do you really, Mother? I mean
(40) are you absolutely crazy in love with it?

**MOTHER:** Oh, yes. It's very cute. . . . (Choking on her words) And there is so much you can do with it.

(45) **CORIE:** I told you she hated it.

**MOTHER:** (Moves toward bedroom landing) Corie, you don't give a person a chance. At least let me see the whole apartment.

(50) **PAUL:** This is the whole apartment.

[Mrs. Banks asks to see the bedroom, and Corie shows her a tiny room at one side of the apartment. Her mother's spirit fails, but she tries to keep a smile
(55) on her face as Corie explains how she is going to use it.]

**MOTHER:** (At bedroom door) That's a wonderful idea. And you can just put a bed in there.

(60) **CORIE:** That's right.

**MOTHER:** How?

[Corie explains that an oversize single will fit in the room, and Mrs. Banks is appalled at the thought of Paul and
(65) Corie sleeping in such cramped conditions. Still she tries not to show her despair.]

**MOTHER:** It's a wonderful idea. Very clever. . . .

(70) **CORIE:** Thank you.

**MOTHER:** Except you can't get to the closet.

**CORIE:** Yes you can.

**MOTHER:** Without climbing over the
(75) bed?

**CORIE:** No, you have to climb over the bed.

**MOTHER:** That's a good idea.

**CORIE:** (Leaves the bedroom, crosses to
(80) ladder and climbs up) Everything's just temporary. As they say in McCall's, it won't really take shape until the bride's own personality becomes more clearly defined.

**GO ON TO THE NEXT PAGE**

17. What has Mrs. Banks had to do in order to visit Corie?

    Mrs. Banks has

    (1)  come from just around the corner
    (2)  had to spend her life savings
    (3)  driven some distance out of her way
    (4)  had to change subways frequently
    (5)  flown in from out of town

18. Which of the following best describes what Mrs. Banks thinks about the bedroom?

    (1)  It is much too small.
    (2)  It is cozy and attractive.
    (3)  It is just the right size.
    (4)  Paul and Corie will enjoy it.
    (5)  Furniture will make it seem larger.

19. Which of the following best describes Paul and Corie?

    (1)  mother and son
    (2)  young newlyweds
    (3)  casual friends
    (4)  brother and sister
    (5)  mother-in-law and son-in-law

20. In this excerpt, how does the author use the size of the bedroom?

    To develop

    (1)  the couple's good judgment in housing
    (2)  Mrs. Banks's view of the couple's situation
    (3)  Corie's skill with interior decorating
    (4)  the author's sympathy for the son-in-law
    (5)  the mother's wealth

**END OF EXAMINATION**

To determine the standard score for the *Official GED Practice Test Form PA: Language Arts, Reading:*

1. Locate the number of questions the candidate answered correctly on the multiple-choice test.
2. Read the corresponding standard score from the column on the right.

Compare the candidate's standard scores to the minimum score requirements in the jurisdiction in which the GED credential is to be issued. (See *Appendix D* in the *Official GED Practice Tests Administrator's Manual*.)

| U.S. Edition Form PA Language Arts, Reading | |
| --- | --- |
| Number of Correct Answers | Estimated GED Test Standard Score |
| 20 | 800 |
| 19 | 650 |
| 18 | 560 |
| 17 | 500 |
| 16 | 470 |
| 16 | 440 |
| 14 | 420 |
| 13 | 410 |
| 12 | 390 |
| 11 | 380 |
| 10 | 370 |
| 9 | 360 |
| 8 | 350 |
| 7 | 340 |
| 6 | 320 |
| 5 | 310 |
| 4 | 280 |
| 3 | 250 |
| 2 | 210 |
| 1 | 200 |

## Language Arts, Reading Answers

1. 2
2. 3
3. 1
4. 1
5. 4
6. 5
7. 1
8. 3
9. 4
10. 3
11. 5
12. 4
13. 5
14. 5
15. 4
16. 3
17. 3
18. 1
19. 2
20. 2

# Pretest Answers and Explanations

1. **(4) the things a person values** The "heart's treasury" is a metaphor for the place where the mind holds treasured memories. The poet makes clear that the memories she holds dear are better than any material or financial wealth. Option (1) is incorrect because there are no other lines in the poem that suggest physical health is the poet's subject. Option (2) is not correct because the "heart's treasury" is not an attitude about time; it is where something—in this case a memory—is kept. Option (3) is incorrect because the poem is not about real money; the references to the treasury, gold, and a coin are examples of figurative language. Option (5) is not correct because the poem contradicts the idea of regret. The poet deeply values her store of memory and expresses no disappointment.

2. **(5) memory of a special experience** Option (5) is correct because the coin is used to symbolize a special memory. The poet makes this point clear in the poem's final two lines: "the safe-kept memory / of a lovely thing." Options (1) and (2) are not correct because the poem does not refer to a lost love or lesson learned, and such memories would probably not be referred to as a "lovely thing." Options (3) and (4) are not correct because nothing in the poem shows progression or growth toward security or wisdom; the poet begins with certainty of what she values. References to the coin, a treasury, gold, and minting are used to symbolize a memory; they are not meant to be literal.

3. **(5) Because of recent Legislature decisions, CareMax had to make changes to their policies.** The paragraph states that the changes "are required by recent bills passed by the Legislature." Option (5) correctly restates this information. For this same reason, option (1) is incorrect; the Legislature passed recent bills that did, in fact, affect your CareMax policy. Option (2) is incorrect because it is a sentence directly from the paragraph and is not broad enough to be a restatement. Option (3) is incorrect because this is a detail of the fourth paragraph, not a restatement of the second paragraph. Option (4) is incorrect because it is based on a misunderstanding of the paragraph; while the legislature does make decisions that could potentially affect insurance, this does not mean that CareMax is a part of the Legislature.

4. **(1) You can now increase your deductible at any time during a year, but only once.** Option (1) correctly summarizes the important points of the paragraph: You can increase your deductible; you can do it at any time; you can only make one change per year. Options (2) and (3) are incorrect because they only contain part of the information presented, and therefore provide only a partial, not complete, summary. Option (4) is incorrect because it is a summary of the first change, not the second. Option (5) is incorrect because you can only increase, not decrease, your deductible once a year.

5. **(4) The Legislature can affect insurance coverage within the United States.** Option (4) is correct. Since the changes to the CareMax policy are a result of Legislative changes, it can be inferred that the Legislature makes decisions that affect insurance. Option (1) is incorrect because this is a detail from the passage, not an inference; it is a direct statement from the passage, so it is not inferred. Option (2) contradicts the passage; you can only change to a higher

deductible, not lower. Option (3) is incorrect because nothing in the passage suggests that the Legislature does not consider your best interests; in fact, allowing members to make changes to their policies at any time during a year is a benefit for members. Option (5) is incorrect and based on a misunderstanding of the passage; a Rider is a document, not your CareMax representative.

6. **(3) Using dry-erase boards will help remedy the main problem of the flexible work schedule.** Option (3) is correct because the main idea of the passage is about implementing the use of white boards in an effort to make scheduling and inter-office communication easier and more efficient. Options (1), (4), and (5) are incorrect because these are details of the passage, not the main idea. Option (2) is incorrect because the flexible work schedule is working; it just needs everyone to work to together to ensure its success.

7. **(2) They are able to balance home and work life more efficiently now.** According to the information presented in the problem, flexible work hours allow "employees to handle the competing demands of work and personal interests." Option (2) is correct because it applies that information to the passage. For this same reason, option (3) and (4) are incorrect; flexible hours would lead to a balance of home and life, not a competition. Options (1) and (5) are incorrect because there is no indication that SYD employees cannot budget time or that they lead busier lives.

8. **(2) We will all enjoy flexible scheduling.** Option (2) is correct because it cannot be proven that all people will enjoy flexible scheduling; since there is no way to be certain that this is a true statement, it is an opinion. Options (1), (3), (4), and (5) are facts from the passage and can be proven to be true.

9. **(3) a mutiny on a ship** Option (3) correctly places the action on a ship. There are many references to a ship (setting), such as captain's cabin, berth, deck, and Turno's plan to throw Aaron overboard. The likelihood that this is a mutiny (plot) comes from the fact that when the men entered the captain's cabin, they wondered if he might rise up and attack them. Option (1) is incorrect because the passage includes no reference to a town, while there is ample evidence in the passage that the action takes place on a ship. Option (2) is not correct because there is no evidence in the passage that the men are soldiers rather than sailors or that they are at war. Option (4) is incorrect because nothing in the passage suggests a city setting. Option (5) is incorrect because the passage includes evidence both of setting (ship) and plot (mutiny).

10. **(3) A narrator describes fictional events occurring in time order.** This option best describes the structure of the passage, which includes narration as well as dialogue, and events are described in the order in which they occur. Option (1) is incorrect because this is not a play—the passage includes description and narration as well as dialogue but does not include stage directions. Option (2) is incorrect because the passage does not make an explicit point and then support it with details, a technique more characteristic of nonfiction. Option (4) is incorrect because causes and effects are not the subject of the passage;

the narrative action is. Option (5) is incorrect because the passage does not take the form of a poem, and nothing suggests the events are metaphorical.

11. **(4) uses their speeches to reveal their different personalities** Option (4) is correct because several characters reveal their natures through the use of their words, which are often given in non-standard English. Option (1) is incorrect because the author does not analyze the personality of any character in the passage. Option (2) is incorrect because, with the exception of Peter trying on the captain's hat, there are no descriptions of the characters' clothing in the passage. Option (3) is incorrect because the narration does not provide the interior thoughts of any character. Option (5) is incorrect because the author gives little physical description of the characters' general appearance.

12. **(1) These are rough people who may turn on each other.** This option best expresses what happens in the passage. Whatever their common goal, this group is clearly rough and already in conflict with each other. Option (2) is not correct because there is not enough information in the passage to tell whether their efforts are doomed to fail or not. Option (3) is incorrect because there is no information in the passage that suggests that Aaron is the cause of any misfortune. Option (4) is incorrect because there is no information that suggests that July is innocent; in fact, he participated in the burglary of the captain's cabin (line 1). Option (5) is not correct because there is no information in the passage that explains why they have taken the actions they have, or whether their course of action is for a good cause.

13. **(3) Hermia loves Lysander while Helena loves Demetrius.** Option (3) correctly states the contrast between the two women. Hermia states that she and Lysander are going to run away together (line 24), and Helena wishes that she looked more like Hermia so that Demetrius would love her back (lines 3–22). Option (1) is incorrect. Hermia does love Lysander, but she does not love Demetrius, as can be seen in how she does not appreciate his attention to her (lines 15–19). Option (2) is incorrect. Demetrius does not love Helena, though she wishes he did. Option (4) is the opposite of the correct answer. Option (5) is incorrect; Lysander loves Hermia.

14. **(1) It makes Demetrius love her more.** Option (1) is correct. Hermia states in line 19 that the more she hates Demetrius, the more he follows her around. Option (2) is incorrect and probably based on a misunderstanding of whom the "he" in line 19 refers to. Options (3), (4), and (5) are incorrect. Hermia's hate mentioned in line 19 does not make others hate her.

15. **(2) her home** Option (2) is correctly identifies the heaven that has been turned to a hell mentioned in line 28. The "heaven" in line 28 refers to the "paradise" of Athens, Hermia's home and the place that Lysander and she are fleeing. Option (1) is incorrect. Though she might be having a hard time with her love life, nothing in the context around line 28 suggest that her youth is like hell to her now. Option (3) is incorrect. Nothing in the passage supports the idea that Hermia's best friend has turned into hell for her. Option

(4) is incorrect. Hermia is running away with her love; he has not turned into hell for her. Option (5) is incorrect. Though her good looks have brought her unwanted attention from another man, she does not lament her beauty at any point in the passage.

16. **(4) plastic surgery to look more like Hermia** Option (4) is correct. Helena wishes that she looked like Hermia (lines 7–14 and 22) so that Demetrius would be in love with her. Option (1) is incorrect. Weight is not mentioned in the passage. Option (2) is incorrect. Nothing in the passage suggests that Hermia is dying of kidney failure. Option (3) is incorrect. Though Helena wishes for new eyes, she wants her eyes to look physically like Hermia's eyes; she does not wish for better vision. Option (5) is incorrect. Though Helena does wish that Hermia's "frowns would teach my smiles such skill," she is wishing her smile would attract Demetrius; no mention of teeth is made.

17. **(5) John doesn't consider others' feelings** Option (5) correctly describes John's treatment of the narrator throughout the passage. She hates the place; he doesn't care. He schedules her life according to what he believes, not what she wants. He hates it when she writes, so she has to hide it from him. His actions show that he is a controlling person with little regard for others. Option (1) is incorrect because John's actions show that he likes to be the person in control and making decisions — he plans the day, picks the room, etc. Option (2) is incorrect because the passage provides no information to suggest that John is either rich or an experienced traveler. Option (3) is not correct because although he picked the room with yellow wallpaper, there is no indication that this is his favorite color. Option (4) is incorrect because there is no evidence to suggest that John ever ran this or any other school for boys.

18. **(1) Some people imprison others while trying to protect them.** This option best expresses the theme of the passage. The narrator gives John credit for trying to be helpful, but he is so domineering that she lives according to his schedule, his taste, his decisions, and his opinions. She keeps her own thoughts to herself. Option (2) is not the best choice because the passage is about the narrator's situation in the relationship; there is no mention of travel, pleasant or unpleasant. Option (3) is not correct because what is troubling the narrator is more than just the physical environment, of which the yellow wallpaper is a part. She is repressed by John. Option (4) is incorrect because the passage is not about the reuse of buildings but about the feelings of repression and loneliness the woman feels. Option (5)—that physical health is all-important—is incorrect because the narrator does not seem very troubled by her health, which is only a minor concern—if a concern at all.

19. **(3) She has conservative tastes.** Option (3) correctly expresses that the narrator has conservative tastes, which are revealed when she notes that the wallpaper pattern commits "every artistic sin" (line 19). Option (1) is not correct because she is a tolerant person, as evidenced by her generosity of feeling toward John. Option (2) is not correct because her judgment in other matters seems reasonable and believable rather than unusual. Option (4) is incorrect because it is precisely the "flamboyant", showy style to

which she objects. Option (5) is not the best choice because there is no evidence in the passage that points to a general preference for solid colors.

20. **(4) privately sad**  Option (4) correctly expresses the tone of the narrator's thoughts. She keeps her thoughts to herself, and she is not happy. She does not express anger (option 1), and she is not at all joyous (option 2). Option (3) is not correct because she is clear in her thoughts and expression, and is confused about nothing. Option (5) is not correct because her narration reveals her innermost thoughts, even though she must hide them from John.

# Answers and Explanations

## Skill 1   Identify the Main Idea
### Pages 12–13

1. **(2) A youth leaving home for the city is surprised that his friend accepts it.** Option (2) correctly shows both what happens and Pip's surprise at Joe's easy ability to deal with it. Option (1) is incorrect because there is nothing that says Pip hates the cattle or that he is definitely going to be married. Option (3) is incorrect because it is clear that Pip and Joe are old friends. Option (4) is incorrect because Joe does not express grief at Pip's leaving, but rather accepts it. Option (5) is incorrect because neither Pip nor Joe expresses in the passage any expectation of Pip sharing his fortune.

2. **(3) Joe is confident in his relationship with Pip.** Option (3) is correct. Joe says so directly in lines 28–29. Option (1) is incorrect because nothing in the passage suggests it's taken a long time for Pip to leave. Option (2) is incorrect. Joe is certain Pip will remember him, as he says in line 29. Option (4) is incorrect because Joe clearly understands what has happened and is not troubled by it, though he will miss Pip. Option (5) is incorrect because Joe never expresses any regret that Pip's life has changed.

3. **(1) Dogs and humans live in different worlds.** Option (1) accurately sums up the details of the passage. Dogs live in a world dominated by scent; humans rely primarily on their eyes. Option (2) is incorrect because dogs perceive an entire world through their noses that is not available to humans. Option (3) is incorrect for the same reason; humans live in a world of sight, but the essay is about differences in perception, not just the abilities of humans. Option (4) is incorrect because the passage is about far more than loving dogs. Option (5) is not the best choice because the passage is about more than the single detail of the dog distrusting its reflection in a mirror.

4. **(4) The narrator frequently tries to get Beau to use his eyes more.** Option (4) is correct because it highlights the difference in how the narrator and Beau use their senses to interact with the world; Beau relies on his sense of smell, but the narrator, who relies on vision, tries to get Beau to use his sense of sight more. Option (1) is incorrect because it highlights a commonality between Beau and the narrator—Beau using his sense of sight—rather than showing the difference. Option (2) is incorrect because the text does not address how the narrator feels about the walks in the woods—this may be another thing they have in common. Options (3) and (5) are not supported by the text.

5. **(3) a main idea implied by details and examples** Option (3) is correct. Eiseley never explicitly says that dogs and humans live in different worlds; instead, he shows us examples and details about what Beau does that is different from what humans do. Option (1) is not the best choice because there is no single sentence that explicitly captures the point of Eiseley's essay. Option (2) is incorrect because the essay is more about ideas than it is about feelings. Option (4) is not the best choice because there is very little in the essay that could be considered a presentation of scientific fact. Option (5) is incorrect because the writer is presenting his ideas, rather than trying to persuade the reader to share a position.

6. **(2) to make readers think about what different living beings experience** Option (2) is correct. Eiseley and Beau live on the same earth, but their experiences in the world are very different; Eiseley intends to show why. Option (1) is incorrect because there is no discussion of the choice of pets. Option (3) is not the best choice because Eiseley is doing more than just praising a dog he likes. Option (4) is incorrect because Eiseley makes no claim that the human mind is better than a dog's. Option (5) is incorrect because the essay does not explore the nature of the ancient relationship between humans and dogs.

## Skill 2   Restate Information
### Pages 16–17

1. **(1) Rocky Rhodes, Builder, and Jane McClean, Contractor, enter into an agreement starting September 27, 2008.** Option (1) correctly restates the information from lines 1 through 7 about the parties to the agreement, their roles, and when the agreement commences. Option (2) is incorrect because it reverses the roles described: Rhodes is the builder and McClean is the contractor. Option (3) is not the best option because it does not restate enough information about who the builder and contractor are and what they are to do. Option (4) is incorrect because the Agreement does not end on September 27; it begins on that date. Option (5) is incorrect because it does not restate information from the paragraph.

2. **(3) The Contractor will supply pest control for residences in Riata Ranch subdivision.** Option (3) accurately reflects the purpose of the entire Agreement. Options (1) and (5) are not the best options because they refer only to details of the agreement rather than restating the contractor's assignment. That the builder will direct the contractor's work when the agreement begins (option 2) is incorrect and does not restate information from the agreement. Option (4) is incorrect because the agreement doesn't have anything to do with the builder completing construction on the residences.

3. **(4) thirty-three cents per square foot or five hundred dollars, whichever is less** Option (4) is correct. The rate is $0.33 per square foot but can never go above $500, the maximum, for a house. Option (1) is not the best answer because it does not include the maximum amount. Option (2) is incorrect because $500 is a maximum rate, not a base rate. Option (3) is incorrect because $500 is the maximum rate and cannot be exceeded. Option (5) is not the best answer because it does not restate the square-foot rate for houses below the maximum.

4. **(3) It is a pleasant evening, but I feel sad.** Option (3) correctly restates that the poet's mood is not lifted by the calmness of the sea or the beauty of the moon, as the "note of sadness" in line 20 indicates. Option (1) is incorrect because the beauty of the evening does not bring the poet peace. Option (2) is incorrect because there is no indication of a coming storm. Option (4) is incorrect because line 1 speaks of a calm sea, and the poet is more sad than worried. Option (5) is incorrect because the poet speaks to someone present, not someone absent, in line 9.

**5. (5) People thousands of years ago felt as we feel.**
Option (5) correctly restates the idea that modern people have the same thoughts as people long ago had about the sound of the sea (lines 21–26). Options (1) and (2) are incorrect because they contradict the poet's direct comparison of the present to the past. Option (3) is incorrect because the poet makes no statement that life has improved. Option (4) is incorrect because the poet says Sophocles felt the same sadness the poet does.

**6. (2) we should take care of each other** Option (2) is correct. In the face of all the sadness he feels, the poet thinks the best we can do is be true to one another. Options (1) and (3) are incorrect because the poem does not include any statement about love conquering all or about anger. Option (4) is incorrect because the poet does not offer much hope in the poem. Option (5) is incorrect because the poet does not address the need to persevere.

**7. (4) Love is all we can be sure of in an uncertain world.** Option (4) is correct; most of the poem is about sadness, but being true to one another in the face of it is what the poet advises. Option (1) is incorrect because the poem does explore the effects of the sea on the poet's thoughts. Option (2) is not the best answer because the sea's eternity is not the point of the poem; what to do in the face of sadness is. Option (3) is incorrect because the poet never addresses the value of learning. Option (5) is not the best choice because the causes of war are not the subject of the poem.

## Skill 3    Summarize Ideas
### Pages 20–21

**1. (3) The appliance should be plugged into a three-prong, fully grounded receptacle.** Option (3) best summarizes the meaning of the first paragraph. Option (1) is not correct because it contradicts information in the paragraph. Option (2) is not correct because it uses "fully eliminates," whereas the paragraph uses the word "minimize" in relation to shock hazard. Option (4) indicates that a receptacle is furnished with the appliance, but that is not true. Option (5) contradicts information in the paragraph that suggests it is the consumer's responsibility to locate and use a grounded receptacle.

**2. (1) You must use the supplied power cord as the manufacturer intended.** Option (1) best summarizes the second paragraph's main point. You need to contact an electrician (option 2) only if the three-prong plug does not fit the desired outlet. Connectors (option 3) are not mentioned in the paragraph at all. Option (4) may be a true statement, but it does not summarize the main idea of the paragraph. Option (5) refers to information from the third paragraph and thus is not a summary of the second paragraph.

**3. (5) The receptacle must provide 115 volts and be properly grounded.** Option (5) best summarizes the main point of the third paragraph. Option (1) provides too many details to be a summary. Options (2), (3), and (4) make inaccurate interpretations of information in the paragraph and are, therefore, not the best summaries.

**4. (4) The narrator gets the superintendent's help, seeks approval from Mrs. Reed, and receives permission to get a new situation.** Option (4) best summarizes the steps that the narrator goes through. Option (1) is not correct because the passage does not indicate that the narrator "secretly" got a job. Option (2) is not correct because the superintendent neither summoned the narrator nor provided a testimonial. Option (3) is not correct because the superintendent did not offer the narrator a job. Option (5) is incorrect because Mr. Brocklehurst did not do any of the listed actions.

**5. (1) The narrator is changing jobs.** Option (1) best summarizes the situation in the passage. That the narrator is being kicked out of Lowood (option 2), that Mr. Brocklehurst has found a new job for the narrator (option 3), or that Mrs. Reed desires that the narrator move to a new situation (option 4) are not correct because they contradict descriptions in the passage. Option (5) may be a true statement, but is not a summary of the situation.

**6. (2) Mrs. Reed does not want to be involved with the narrator.** Option (2) best summarizes Mrs. Reed's reply. Option (1) is not correct because the passage states Mrs. Reed had given up "all interference." Option (3) is incorrect because Mrs. Reed indicates that the narrator may do as she pleases; Mrs. Reed does not withhold permission. Option (4) is not correct because Mrs. Reed neither confirms nor denies that she is the narrator's guardian. Option (5) is not correct because it contradicts the statement in lines 23 and 24 that she had "relinquished all interference" in the narrator's affairs.

## Skill 4    Identify Implications
### Pages 24–25

**1. (4) scientific knowledge** Option (4) best summarizes the implication of "learn'd"; the charts, diagrams, and proofs support the idea. Option (1) is the opposite of the correct answer. The details of the poem imply that scientific knowledge does not necessarily equal great wisdom. Options (2), (3), and (5) are incorrect because nothing in the poem supports the idea that the term "learn'd astronomer" suggests religious tradition, literary expertise, or native folklore.

**2. (1) He finds the lecture boring and repetitious.** Option (1) is the best answer. The repetition of "When" echoes the boring repetition of the lecture. As the rest of the poem implies, the lecturer's knowledge (option 2) is unsatisfying to the poet. While the subject of astronomy is truly vast, option (3) is not the best choice. The repetition of the "When" clauses implies less about the vastness of astronomy than what the poet identifies as the lecture's tedious and unsatisfying nature. The implication that the lecture was fast-paced and interesting (option 4) is incorrect and not supported by the details of the poem. Option (5) is incorrect. The poet's repetitions of "When" imply boredom or fatigue rather than a well-organized subject matter.

**3. (4) It cannot explain everything.** Option (4) is correct. By comparing the tedium of the lecture to the mystery of the stars, the poet implies there are limits on human scientific knowledge. Option (1) is incorrect and contradicted by the poem, which has little praise for scientific learning. Option (2) is incorrect because the poem does not make value comparisons between scientific knowledge and poetry. Option (3) is not the best answer. While the poem suggests the lecturer's fame ("much applause in the lecture room"), the stronger implication is that the lecturer's knowledge and fame are tiresome and inadequate. Option (5) is incorrect; scientific knowledge, the poem implies, is less entertaining than the mystery of the night sky.

4. **(3) It is inadequate.** Option (3) is the best choice because the poem implies the inability of science to fully describe the mystery of the stars. Option (1) is incorrect because the poet does not imply that science is wrong, just that it is insufficient. Option (2) is incorrect. Nothing in the poem supports the implication that human knowledge is of great interest. Option (4) is incorrect. The text does not imply that human knowledge must be well structured. Option (5) is incorrect. The poem implies the lecturer had a large audience ("much applause") and that the poet is unique in his lack of interest.

5. **(4) Words are too limited to describe or measure it.** Option (4) is correct. The silence of the outside air is contrasted with the great amount of talking going on inside the lecture hall, implying that no amount of talking can adequately describe or measure the universe. Options (1) and (2) are not implied; the astronomer does not know all there is to know, and the poet's "sickness" is a result of the experience in the lecture, not the cause of his distaste. Option (3) is not correct. Nothing in the poem implies that human nature is important. Nothing in the poem supports the implication that the stars are less important than any other part of the universe (option 5).

6. **(1) People did not start sandbagging early enough in previous years.** Option (1) correctly identifies the implication. The writer notes that early sandbagging "This year" will help and points to the need to start early, implying that they didn't start early enough in previous years. Options (2) and (3) are not implied; nowhere does the passage say there weren't enough sandbags or that no sandbagging was done last year. Option (4) is incorrect; the writer wants to change the sandbagging start to when the hurricane is reported, implying that in previous years residents waited until later. Option (5) is not correct because there is no information of any kind that implies when the last hurricane was.

7. **(3) In previous years, Sea Breeze had to wait for more supplies from other areas.** Option (3) is implied because the writer doesn't want to have to "depend on outside help this year," a change from previous years. Option (1) is not implied; the writer says the supplies were short, not absent. Options (2) and (4) are not correct; the passage doesn't mention or refer to funding or to where supplies will be stored. Nothing implies Sea Breeze distributed supplies to other towns (option 5).

8. **(2) The town wants to improve its emergency response.** Option (2) is correct. The entire purpose of the message is to highlight ways to improve emergency response. Option (1) is not implied because every point in the text is about making improvement. Options (3), (4), and (5) are incorrect because the text contains nothing to imply anything about the likelihood of hurricanes this year, past injuries, or how frequently the town is hit by hurricanes.

## Skill 5 Get Meaning from Context
### Pages 28–29

1. **(3) entirely** Option (3) is the correct choice. The passage first describes the matrons in the middle distance, then the description moves to the foreground, which is filled entirely with young girls. Options (1), (2), and (4) are not supported by the context. There is nothing to indicate a time reference ("today"), that the situation is temporary, or that the girls are in any order. Likewise, there is nothing in the passage to suggest the location of the young girls is unfair (option 5).

2. **(3) slender** Option (3) is correct. The context indicates that the girls' forms were *not* sylph because their contours were "robust and solid," so "slender" is the logical choice. Option (1) is not correct because the context says exactly the opposite. Option (2) is not correct because the health of the girls is not mentioned or in question. Nothing in the context indicates that *sylph* means "proud" (option 4). Option (5) is not correct because "white" describes what the forms were wearing, not the forms themselves.

3. **(5) companion** Option (5) is correct. The context indicates that the narrator and the girl were eating together, so "companion" is the logical choice. Option (1) is not logical because a waitress would not have been eating with the narrator. Option (2) is redundant; the narrator has already said that the girl was her student. Options (3)—governess—and (4)—entertainer—are meanings not supported in the context of the passage.

4. **(1) They were dull and lacked manners.** Option (1) is supported by the narrator's comment about the girls' brains in lines 30 and 31, and by the tale of the girl who ate so much and pocketed what she could not eat. That they were the best, brightest students the narrator had known (option 2) is contradicted in the context of details about their brains never having got them far in the past and the difficulty of teaching them now. Options (3) and (4) are not correct because the narrator does not comment on the figures of the girls she knew, nor on their values or dresses. Option (5) describes a feeling that is more negative than the context and details of the passage indicate.

5. **(1) other devices that are connected to a computer** Option (1) is clearly indicated by the examples, "such as a printer, keyboard, or mouse." The other options are incorrect. Other details in the passage clearly contradict that peripherals are unimportant or unnecessary devices (option 2), the parts of the computer that store information (option 3), software programs (option 4), or parts of the computer that alert you to problems (option 5).

6. **(3) damaged (line 8)** Option (3) is the word most closely related to *frayed* and gives a clue about its meaning. The other options are incorrect; "connections" (option 1), "tight" (option 2) "cables" (option 3), and "installed" (option 4) do not give clues to the meaning of *frayed*.

7. **(2) making sure something is correct** Option (2) is the correct meaning, as indicated in context by the sentences that follow (lines 16–23). Option (1)—disconnect— is not supported by context. Neither option (3) nor option (4)—installing new equipment or registering—makes sense in context. Option (5) is incorrect; nothing in the passage supports a meaning related to counting and measuring.

8. **(3) a program that finds problems with the computer** Option (3) is correct; the context indicates that readers should consult the diagnostics chapter if they have a persistent problem. Options (1) and (2) are incorrect because

they do not make sense within the chapter title referenced: "Running the Powermax Diagnostics." Option (4) is not correct because the context indicates that readers should consult the diagnostics if they have a persistent problem, not if they need to register. Option (5) makes no sense in the context of the passage.

## Skill 6   Apply Ideas to a New Context
### Pages 32–33

1. **(4) the way things change over time** Option (4) is correct. Twain compares the world he knew as a boy to the way the world is now, a comparison everyone can apply. Option (1) is not the best choice; the passage includes no information about how much the town has grown. Option (2) is incorrect because Twain expresses no regret over things he did when he was young. Option (3) is not the best choice because Twain acknowledges from the hilltop the natural beauty of the surrounding area. Option (5) is not the best choice because Twain does not focus as much on changes in himself as on changes in the people of the town.

2. **(1) that part of him wishes he could preserve the world as it was** Option (1) best suggests an interpretation of Twain's dreams that could apply to his attitude about time. This can be seen in that he remembers people as they had been instead of how they actually look now. Option (2) is not a correct answer, because while Twain may be troubled by the aging of the townspeople, he is not in the least confused by it. Option (3) cannot be applied to Twain's dreams because Twain stops short of claiming that the past was better; he feels old but does not say that earlier days were better ones. Option (4) does not apply; Twain makes no statement about having wasted his youth. Option (5) is not the best choice. Acceptance of aging does not apply to the dreams Twain had; he is in fact troubled by the years his mind travels from the past to the present when he awakens.

3. **(5) The world changes whether we want it to or not.** Option (5) is correct. Much like the people and places that had changed for Twain, people and places change with time in the real world, too. Option (1) is not the best choice. People do change in Twain's essay; they physically grow old. Option (2) is not the best choice. It may be good advice, but it cannot be determined from the essay, as he makes no claim that either present or past is better. Option (3) is not the best application of Twain's ideas from the essay because he does not take comfort in childhood memories. They remind him only of the distance between then and now. Option (4) is not the best choice because Twain does not say whether he regrets or is glad he revisited Hannibal.

4. **(2) seek to improve one's mind** Option (2) is the best application of Thoreau's thoughts on consciously elevating one's life. Thoreau lives a life of the mind. Option (1) is not the best application of Thoreau's idea because he makes no recommendation in the passage of meeting different people. Option (3) is not a good choice because there is no hint in the passage that to "elevate" has anything to do with material wealth. Option (4) is not the best choice; Thoreau's idea of "awakening" is about the mind. Option (5) is not the best choice because Thoreau's intention is to raise one's mental focus, not physical shape.

5. **(4) by living without thinking much about it** Option (4) is correct. The application of Thoreau's message is for everyone to think about why one does anything and whether it is of high purpose. Option (1) is not the best choice because Thoreau does not state whether he dislikes or enjoys the company of others, but he does value his own self-examination more. Options (2) and (3) are incorrect because Thoreau makes no comment on physical health nor on beauty in the environment; both are valuable, but they are not applications of Thoreau's ideas as expressed here. Option (5) is also incorrect. Thoreau makes no mention of the consequences of dying young.

6. **(4) find something to do that he cared about** Option (4) is correct. Thoreau's ideas here suggest that what one does not care about is not worth doing. Option (1) is not the best choice; in lines 16–19 Thoreau expresses impatience at putting up with things of no value, such as a job that makes a person unhappy. Option (2) would not be a good application of Thoreau's ideas because although he might advise quitting something trivial, he would never advise waiting for something to come along. Instead, he talks about affecting "the quality of the day" as being "the highest of arts" (lines 15–16). There is no support for the idea of confrontation with others in the passage (option 3). Giving up caring (option 5) would never satisfy Thoreau; everyone is "tasked to make his life, even in its details" all that it might be.

7. **(3) that he wants every day to matter** Option (3) best applies Thoreau's thought that he wants to know life "by experience" in order to gain the truest understanding of it. Option (1) is not correct. Thoreau does not mention reading as a way of truly knowing life. The passage makes no reference to traveling as a way to improve oneself (option 2). Nothing in the passage suggests Thoreau will become more certain with age (option 4) or that he is uncertain of his views as they exist (option 5).

## Skill 7   Make Inferences
### Pages 36–37

1. **(3) She takes pride in doing things herself.** Option (3) is a good inference about Mrs. Lopez, who rents a machine to do a job herself rather than hiring someone else to do it. Option (1) is incorrect. Nothing indicates she complains a lot. Option (2) has no support in the passage; she is working in the yard, but there is no indication that she does this a lot. Option (4) is not a reasonable inference; there is no indication of how frequently she shops. Option (5) contradicts the very fact that Mrs. Lopez wrote the letter to express her thoughts.

2. **(4) He is sensitive to his customers' feelings.** Option (4) is correct based on the way that Dave speaks and acts while helping Mrs. Lopez. Options (1), (2), and (5) are not reasonable inferences because there is no evidence in the passage to indicate how long he has worked there, whether he is up for promotion, or his age. Option (3) is not the best choice because Dave urges Mrs. Lopez to use the machine.

3. **(2) He knows where Mrs. Lopez lives.** Option (2) is a correct inference based on Joe's statement that "Dave is doing some repairs in your neighborhood." Options (1) and (4)—Joe is using a cell phone and Davis is his best friend—are not reasonable inferences based on the passage. Option (3) is not

the best choice; Joe explains how to start the stump grinder, which indicates that he has probably used it. That Joe loves his job (option 5) is not mentioned in the passage.

4. **(1) It has a gas-powered engine.** Option (1) is a reasonable inference given that Mrs. Lopez "pulled a rope" to start the machine and "the engine caught." Option (2) is not the best option because Mrs. Lopez was able to unload and position the machine by herself, which indicates it is a one-person job. Option (3) is not the best choice; there is no indication that other customers have had trouble with the machine. Options (4) and (5) are not reasonable; there is no evidence in the passage that the tool's blades are dull or that it comes in different sizes.

5. **(2) They had similar views on life.** Option (2) is consistent with many statements in the passage. Option (1) is not a reasonable inference; nothing in the passage suggests the four people are siblings. Option (3) is not correct; the passage indicates that the people are aging (27–28), but not that they are ill. Option (4) is incorrect and contradicted by the passage; the author knows things about the others' lives a stranger wouldn't know. Option (5) is not the best choice; though the passage mentions "our hottest arguments," it does not indicate that they argued continuously.

6. **(2) thoughtful** Option (2) is the best inference about the narrator, based on his careful analysis of his youth and the ideals and values of "the foursome." Option (1) is not correct because in line 42 he refers to his youthful optimism, but the message is that he is no longer as optimistic as he once was. Options (3) and (5)—shallow and simple—are incorrect inferences that are the opposite of the correct choice. Option (4) does not present a reasonable inference; the narrator's views are not envious.

7. **(1) He is somewhat disappointed in his life.** Option (1) is a reasonable inference based on the narrator's opening sentence. Option (2) is not supported in the passage; the narrator's accomplishments are not listed or commented upon, other than in the abstract. Option (3) is not a reasonable inference; the narrator does not state plans for the future. Option (4) is not correct; it contradicts lines 7–9, in which the narrator says that he knew they did not have the "gifts to reorder society." Option (5) is not correct; it contradicts lines, 44–45, in which the narrator says that "I can't charge myself with real ill will."

## Skill 8  Identify Causes and Effects
## Pages 40–41

1. **(5) Big Earl's job was to scout basketball players.** Option (5) is correct. Lines 23–24 show that Earl is a basketball scout, which causes him to track down Arthur. Option (1) is incorrect because the passage does not say that Big Earl wants to take Arthur to see the skyscrapers. Options (2), (3), and (4) are incorrect because no details in the passage support the statements that Arthur's mother sent Big Earl to bring Arthur home, that Arthur had invited Big Earl to play with him, or that Big Earl did not like Arthur playing basketball with older boys. Thus, these cannot be causes of Big Earl seeking Arthur at the basketball courts.

2. **(4) Arthur was a better player than most boys his age.** Option (4) is correct. Arthur is good enough to draw a scout to watch him. This is a clue that Arthur is an especially good player for his age and size. Option (1) is not the most likely cause of Arthur's playing against older boys; the passage describes a neighborhood with many children and there is nothing in the passage to suggest that Arthur wasn't popular with those his own age. Option (2) cannot be the cause; the passage includes no details that suggest Arthur was forced to play. Option (3) is incorrect because Earl's wish to see Arthur play is not the reason that Arthur was playing against older boys. There is nothing to suggest that being called a runt (option 5) caused Arthur to play the older boys; rather, it was likely an effect of him playing against the bigger boys.

3. **(4) Kids played in the streets and around the tenements.** Option (4) is correct. The fact that kids played in the street is an effect of poverty because it means that they did not have yards or parks to play in. The fact that they lived in tenements is also an effect of poverty. Options (1) and (3) are details about the temperature of the day and Big Earl's dreams, neither of which would result from the neighborhood's poverty. Option (2) is a detail that describes wealth just beyond the neighborhood, but the skyscrapers of glass and steel are not an effect of the neighborhood's poverty. Option (5) is a detail that could describe both rich and poor neighborhoods, so it cannot be an effect of the neighborhood's poverty.

4. **(1) The person will have allergy symptoms.** Option (1) is correct. The central idea of the passage is that dark-furred cats cause allergy symptoms in people who are allergic to cats. Option (2) is incorrect; sneezing is an allergy symptom, and a black cat is likely to cause, not prevent, allergy symptoms. Option (3) is incorrect because the passage states that few allergy sufferers get rid of their pets. Option (4) is incorrect because while the first line of the passage says having a black cat may be bad luck after all, the author does not mean for readers to take the statement literally; the idea of bad luck is a superstition and is not a real effect. Option (5) is incorrect. A person who has allergy symptoms may need medicine, but the passage does not say so.

5. **(5) antigens** Option (5) is correct. In lines 17–18, the doctor who is quoted says that antigens make people sneeze. Option (1) is incorrect because the passage does not suggest that fur causes sneezing. Option (2) is incorrect. Dust may cause some people to sneeze, but it is not the cause of sneezing in people who are allergic to and exposed to cats. Option (3) is incorrect because lines 16–18 explain that sebum causes sneezing only indirectly by producing antigens. Option (4) is incorrect. The article mentions bathing cats but does not say that bathing—cats or people—causes sneezing.

6. **(2) dark-furred cats causing allergy symptoms but light-furred cats not** Option (2) is correct. In lines 13–14, the doctor who led the study says that he does not know why dark cats cause a problem for allergy sufferers. Option (1) is incorrect because the article does not discuss the cause of some people having allergies and others not having them. Option (3) is incorrect. The article says that few allergy sufferers get rid of their pets, but this is not something that researchers studied. Option (4) is incorrect because the article makes clear that researchers do know some of the causes of allergy symptoms improving (bathing cats and keeping them away from bedrooms). Option (5) is incorrect. The article

does not discuss whether researchers know the cause of this behavior.

**7. (2) A person with allergies will have fewer symptoms.** Option (2) is correct. Lines 20–21 state that allergy symptoms can be reduced by bathing cats weekly. Option (1) is incorrect; the article does not say that reduced shedding is an effect of bathing a cat. Option (3) is not the best choice because the article does not confirm that a weekly cat bath will have the effect of limiting allergy development. The emphasis is on reducing symptoms. Options (4) and (5) are incorrect. The article does not say that bathing a cat will have the effect of a cat either staying away from bedrooms or producing more sebum.

## Skill 9   Distinguish Fact and Opinion
### Pages 44–45

**1. (5) The production is award winning.** Option (5) is correct. Lines 43–44 state that the production has won Tony Awards. This is a fact that can be proven. That the music is disappointing (option 1), the lyrics pleasant (option 2), the performer who plays Amneris convincing (option 3), and the performer who plays Aida outstanding (option 4) are incorrect because they are all opinions—statements that cannot be proven true and that others may disagree with.

**2. (5) Everyone should see the production.** Option (5) is correct. In line 46, the author urges readers to "get your ticket." This makes clear his belief that everyone should see the production. This is an opinion because it cannot be proven true, and others may disagree with it. That the show opened in 2000 (option 1); that it features new music (option 2); that two artists designed the sets, costumes, and lighting (option 3); and that the characters include two princesses (option 4) are incorrect because they are all facts—statements that can be proven true and that leave no room for disagreement.

**3. (2) He is impressed with the set designers but not with the composers.** Option (2) is correct. In lines 23–27, the author uses the words "disappointment," "strident," "uninspiring" and "not memorable" to express his opinion of the work of the composers. In lines 12–20, he repeatedly praises the work of the designers, showing that he is impressed with them. Options (1) and (3) are incorrect because the author's opinions as explained above are exactly the opposite of what is stated. Options (4) and (5) are incorrect because they do not reflect the author's clearly stated opinions that the composers are a disappointment while the set designers did excellent work.

**4. (2) She likes to be around people.** Option (2) is correct. In line 16, Mrs. Rachel says, "I'd ruther look at people" than live in a secluded house surrounded by trees. The fact that she likes to be around people can be proven by Mrs. Rachel's own words and by her actions. Option (1) is incorrect because it is an opinion about Mrs. Rachel, not a fact. Option (3) is incorrect because the passage does not tell whether Mrs. Rachel is Irish. That Mrs. Rachel is a snob (option 4) or too nosy (option 5) are incorrect because they are opinions that cannot be proven true, and some people may disagree with them.

**5. (4) It was remote and unappealing.** Option (4) is correct. The idea that Green Gables was unappealing is Mrs.

Rachel's opinion; it is not a fact that can be proven true. Not everyone believes that the house is unappealing; in line 17, Mrs. Rachel acknowledges that the Cuthberts seem content living at Green Gables. Options (1), (2), and (3)—that Green Gables was built on the edge of a clearing, nearly hidden from the road, and unlike the neighboring houses—are incorrect because they are facts about the house that can be proven true. The statement in option (5) is also a fact based on statements in the passage about how many trees there were (lines 13–16).

**6. (1) strange** Option (1) is correct. In line 12, Mrs. Rachel gives her opinion that the Cuthberts are "a little odd." Option (2) is not the best answer because while Mrs. Rachel implies that she would be lonely if she lived at Green Gables, she does not say that the Cuthberts are lonely there. Instead she says in line 17 that they "seem contented." Options (3), (4), and (5) are incorrect because no details in the passage support the idea that Mrs. Rachel thinks that the Cuthberts are poor, mean, or dishonest.

**7. (3) She is impressed by its neatness.** Option (3) is correct. Lines 26–34 describe the neatness and cleanliness of the backyard and Mrs. Rachel's opinion that Mrs. Cuthbert must clean the yard as often as she cleans the house. Option (1) is incorrect because no details in the passage support the idea that Mrs. Rachel thinks the yard is too large. Options (2) and (4) are not the best answers because while Mrs. Rachel holds the opinions that the house is too secluded and that it has too many trees, these are comments that relate to the house in general, not only the yard. That Mrs. Rachel thinks the yard is dirty (option 5) is incorrect because it is the opposite of what is stated in the text (lines 26–34).

## Skill 10   Interpret Symbols and Imagery
### Pages 48–49

**1. (2) religious conviction** Option (2) is the best choice because the wife's name, "Faith," brings the issue of religion into the passage. Brown worries about leaving "Faith behind." She is also referred to as a "blessed angel." Option (1) is not the best choice because Brown is leaving only his home, not all of society, and he is more concerned about Faith than anyone else. Option (3) is not the best choice because the issue of Brown's love for his wife is less important than his thoughts of her as an angel and a path to heaven. Option (4) is not correct because Brown's wife is not selfless and does not want him to leave, nor does he wish to go. Option (5) is not correct, because Faith's goodness would be an unlikely symbol for selfishness.

**2. (1) sight** Option (1) is correct because the words *dreary, darkened, gloomiest,* and *narrow* all appeal primarily to the sense of sight. Options (2), (3), (4), and (5) are not correct because the words in the lines do not appeal to senses of hearing, taste, touch, or smell.

**3. (2) a growing sense of dread** Option (2) is the best choice. The dreary road, the gloomy trees, and the narrow path create a "dark" feeling. Options (1) and (3) are not correct because Brown's grim errand does not show any sense of adventure or excitement. Option (4) is not correct because the solitude Brown feels is ominous, or scary, rather than tender. Option (5) is not correct because Brown does not show any sense of peacefulness or absence from worry.

4. **(4) an exploration of uncertainty** Option (4) is the best choice because Brown is on his way to an unknown, and the images and actions support this idea as a symbol of his journey. Option (1) is not correct because while nature is mentioned in the forest he travels through, he is not battling it. Option (2) is not correct because nothing in Brown's actions or thoughts show any question of his love for his wife. Option (3) is not the best choice for what is symbolized, as Brown goes about his errand with a heavy heart rather than a sense of freedom. Option (5) is not symbolized—Brown shows no sense of optimism.

5. **(4) "The long stretches of the waterway ran on, deserted, into the gloom of overshadowed distances."** Option (4) appeals to the sense of sight with phrases like "long stretches," "deserted," and "gloom of overshadowed distances." Options (1) and (5) are incorrect because there are no visual descriptions in those sentences. Option (2) is incorrect because the warm, thick, heavy air is felt, not seen. Option (3) is incorrect because the "noisy dream" suggests the sense of hearing.

6. **(2) the feeling of the air** Option (2) is correct. Feeling is a part of the sense of touch, and he describes the air as "warm, thick, heavy..." which signify touch. Option (1) is not correct because the length of the river is more a sense of sight and time than touch. Option (3) is not correct because the dangers cannot be felt. Option (4) is not correct because the narrator's fatigue is a mental state caused by his stress at watching for danger. Option (5) is not correct because it refers directly to the sense of sight, not touch.

7. **(4) the ancient, mysterious past** Option (4) is correct. Throughout the passage, the narrator comments on the sense of entering an almost prehistoric world (lines 1–4 and 27–29). The river symbolizes the untamed world of the past. Option (1) is not correct because the river is separate from the world of the narrator and does not represent any indecision he might feel. Option (2) is not correct because the river does not seem to stand for anything related to human effort to live a good life. Option (3) is not correct because there is no reference to aging or the life cycle. Option (5) is also not the best choice because the narrator does not discuss his goals in life.

## Skill 11 Interpret Figurative Language
Pages 52–53

1. **(2) sat motionless on the ground** Option (2) best expresses the simile that creates an image of a harmless thing that stays in one place. Option (1) is not the best choice; the rabbit was already visible. Option (3) is incorrect; nothing in the simile indicates the rabbit's age. Option (4) is incorrect; nothing in the passage suggests that the rabbit is dead. Option (5) is not the best choice; nothing in the simile or image suggests that a rabbit or a flower would be out of place in the courtyard.

2. **(1) ran with great speed** Option (1) is correct. The simile suggests the speed of a bullet. Option (2) is not correct because the simile is describing how the rabbit ran, and it did not run as if wounded. Option (3) is incorrect because a rabbit would not make noise as it ran. Option (4) is incorrect because the rabbit ran "round and round"; the simile applies to the

rabbit's speed, not its direction. The simile is describing the rabbit's manner of running and gives no indication of what it might be feeling (option 5).

3. **(2) "like a furry meteorite"** Option (2) is the only one of the five choices that uses the words *like* or *as* to make a comparison. Option (1) is not a simile; it is a phrase that describes the rabbit's motion and it makes no comparison. Option (3) is not a simile but a prepositional phrase; it describes how the rabbit ran. Option (4) is not a simile but a dependent clause; it describes the effect of the rabbit's circling. Option (5) is not a simile but a verb and adverb from a different sentence.

4. **(5) simile to describe the rabbit's flight** Option (5) is correct. The word *like* indicates that the phrase makes a simile. Option (1) is incorrect because the words are not a metaphor, which labels one thing as another to make a comparison without using *like* or *as*. Option (2) is not the best choice because there is no indication in the passage that Gudrun is in a bad mood. Option (3) is incorrect because the words do not make a metaphor and there is no comparison between fear and anger. Option (4) is incorrect because the phrase is not about actual weather; it is a simile that compares the violence of the rabbit's dash to a storm.

5. **(4) similes** Option (4) is correct. A simile uses the words *like* or *as* to make a comparison, and the speaker uses *like* in every phrase but one. Option (1) is not correct; the descriptive words are similes making comparisons, not simple descriptions. Option (2) is incorrect; metaphors do not use the word *like* to make comparisons. Option (3) is not the best choice; the language consists of similes, not merely sensory language by itself, though sensory language is used to construct the similes. Option (5) is not correct because the words are not the reported words of a speaker set off in quotation marks.

6. **(4) a deep feeling of romantic attraction** Option (4) is correct. All of the similes express or create an image of an appealing, powerful, or sudden feeling, and in lines 38–39 the speaker says these things happened "when you gave me that first long look across the room," an indication of attraction. Option (1) is not correct because the similes and their images do not suggest negative experiences. Options (2) and (3) are not the best choices because the similes express comparisons to experience, rather than a desire for something new or in the future. Option (5) is not the best choice because the similes are all comparisons to the feeling the speaker got when someone attractive looked at him. Although the comparisons themselves are varied, what they express is a single comparison, rather than contradictions and complexities.

7. **(5) a feeling of wonder and awe** Option (5) is correct. The simile describes the feeling one might get on a warm night looking up at the moon; it is consistent with the other positive similes in the passage. Option (1) is not correct; the simile and the context of the passage do not suggest coldness. Option (2) is incorrect; there is nothing in the simile to suggest either eeriness or hesitation. Option (3) is incorrect; the simile and the rest of the passage show that these feelings are vitally important to the speaker. Option (4) is not correct; the simile and the context of the rest of the passage suggest a full heart, not an empty one.

8. **(2) sudden thrill** Option (2) is correct. The plunge into the cold water that the simile describes would be an invigorating experience, a sudden thrill. Option (1) is not the best choice because *descent* suggests decline, which is not consistent with the feelings described. Option (3) is not the best choice; the simile describes the feeling of entering the water more than the courage it takes to dive. Option (4) is not the best choice; the simile intends to describe a sudden pleasure, not an achievement. Option (5) is not correct; there is nothing to suggest the diver is out of control as he or she enters the water.

9. **(3) scene of exotic excitement** Option (3) is correct. The simile describes the color and attraction of the electrifying view of nightlife. Option (1) is not the best choice; the simile does not suggest either blindness or confusion. Option (2) is not correct; the speaker is excited, not threatened. Option (4) is not correct; the simile suggests the adventure of the city at night, not waste or loss. Option (5) is not correct; the simile suggests pleasure, not annoyance.

10. **(1) something clean and refreshing** Option (1) is correct. The aroma of pine trees in a forest suggests clean air, unspoiled nature. Options (2), (3), (4), and (5) are not good choices; they all have negative connotations, while the simile and the rest of the passage indicate that the comparison is positive rather than negative.

## Skill 12 Analyze Characterization
## Pages 56–57

1. **(4) He is disconnected from reality.** Option (4) is the best answer. Quixote believes what he reads in his books is real, which leads him to lose his wits and decide to become a knight himself. Options (1) and (2) are not correct because the description reveals nothing of bitterness or envy in the character. Option (3) is not the best choice because Quixote dreams of adventure and "righting every kind of wrong," not of war. Option (5) is not correct because the description reveals nothing of fear or suspicion in the character.

2. **(4) They fill his head full of fanciful and absurd ideas.** Option (4) is correct. The passage indicates that Don Quixote believes the characters and events in the books he reads are real, which leads him to attempt to emulate them. Option (1) is not correct because nothing in the passage indicates that Quixote has become an enchanter. Option (2) is not correct; Quixote's housekeeper and niece are mentioned, but the passage does not say that he ran off with them. Option (3) is not correct because the passage does not say that Quixote wrote stories. Option (5) is incorrect because the passage does not indicate where Quixote's fancy will lead.

3. **(1) fanciful and imaginative** Option (1) is correct. Quixote is so obsessed with his fantastic ideas that his sense of reality is distorted, as in a dream. Option (2) is not correct because the passage does not say that Quixote writes stories. Option (3) is not correct because in the passage Quixote takes no action that indicates he is dangerous. Option (4) is not correct because the passage indicates neither Quixote's age nor what his youthful ambitions might have been. Option (5) is not correct because the passage suggests that he lives with his housekeeper and niece.

4. **(2) The author describes him.** Option (2) is correct. The author describes Don Quixote in great detail, including his obsession with knight stories and his goal to "make a knight-errant of himself." Option (1) is incorrect because Don Quixote does not speak in the passage; all the description comes from the author. Option (3) is incorrect because there is no dialogue in the passage. Option (4) is not correct because the passage does not include any of Don Quixote's thoughts. While we do learn *about* his thoughts, it is because the narrator describes what Quixote is thinking. Option (5) is incorrect. The author tells us what Don Quixote wants to do in the future, but we do not actually see any of his actions in the present.

5. **(4) he privately criticizes himself harshly** Option (4) paraphrases lines 8–10, which state that Doctor Sloper "escaped all criticism but his own." Option (1) restates the narrator's opinion of the doctor (stated in line 3), not the doctor's opinion of himself. Option (2) describes the doctor's relationship with his daughter, not how the doctor feels about himself. Options (3) and (5) state what other people think of the doctor or how they behave toward him, not how the doctor feels about himself.

6. **(4) Though disappointed that she is a girl, he is determined to raise her well.** Lines 26–30 support option (4). No details in the passage support options (1) or (3). Option (2) contradicts the statement that he decided "to make the best of her." Option (5) is not correct because the passage describes the child as "robust and healthy," not as wild.

7. **(1) unforgiving** Option (1) is correct. Lines 8–16 show that Doctor Sloper never forgave himself for the deaths of his wife and son. Options (2) and (5) are incorrect; nothing in the passage suggests that the doctor is frightening or immature. Option (3) is incorrect. Though he is a popular doctor, the passage does not suggest this is so because he is charming, but rather because people found his misfortune fascinating. Option (4) is incorrect. Lines 22–23 suggest that the doctor's wife and son died of a deadly disease; there is nothing to suggest they died because Sloper was careless.

## Skill 13 Interpret Plot and Setting
## Pages 60–61

1. **(1) the narrator's office** Option (1) is correct. The narrator calls it an office in lines 7 and 24. Option (2) is incorrect because the narrator makes clear that Bartleby is at the narrator's place. Option (3) is incorrect; the reference to the mid-Atlantic is just an expression to suggest Bartleby's drifting nature. Option (4) is incorrect because Bartleby apparently has no home. Option (5) is incorrect because the narrator makes it clear that the property is his office (lines 7 and 24).

2. **(4) the past** Option (4) is correct. The exact time period is unspecified, but the verb tense and the style suggest the past. Option (1) is incorrect because there is no information to suggest an ancient setting. Option (2) is incorrect because nothing in the passage specifies a certain era. Option (3) is incorrect. The narrator told Bartleby he must leave the office in six days' time, but the passage doesn't make clear how this detail relates to the time setting of the story. Option (5) is incorrect because both the verb tense and the style suggest the past.

3. **(2) Bartleby will not leave the narrator's office.**
Option (2) is correct. This is the problem the narrator
approaches throughout the passage. Option (1) is incorrect
because the copying, or ceasing of it, is not what bothers
the narrator. Option (3) is not supported by the passage; the
reference to the mid-Atlantic is an expression about Bartleby's
solitude. Option (4) is not correct because there is no indication
that the narrator fears or has discovered theft. Option (5) is
incorrect because the narrator expresses no anxiety about his
business; he only notes that he must attend to it.

4. **(1) He does nothing.** Option (1) is correct. Bartleby
quits copying and "would do nothing in the office" (lines
6–7). Option (2) is incorrect because he may have copied
documents at some time, but he has quit (line 1). Option (3)
is incorrect; the reference to the millstone is not about the
business—it is an expression indicating that the narrator feels
weighed down by Bartleby's presence. Option (4) is incorrect
because the narrator says that Bartleby "would do nothing
in the office." Option (5) is incorrect because there is no
indication in the text that Bartleby writes letters.

5. **(5) inside a courtyard at night** Option (5) is correct.
Romeo has climbed the orchard walls to see Juliet. She does
not know he is inside until he announces himself. Option (1) is
incorrect because there is no reference to a forest. Option (2)
is incorrect because they are clearly inside a walled enclosure,
not on a street. Option (3) is incorrect because he has been
able to "o'erperch" the walls and is inside. Option (4) is incorrect
because there are several references to darkness and night.

6. **(3) Juliet's family wants to kill Romeo.** Option (3)
correctly identifies the conflict revealed in this scene. Juliet
warns Romeo that her family will kill him if they find him there
(lines 21–23 and 31–32). Option (1) is incorrect. The problem
is not that Romeo loves Juliet; the problem is that their families
are warring and hate each other. Options (2), (4), and (5) are
incorrect and contradicted by the text: Juliet does not hate
Romeo, Romeo did make it past the walls, and Juliet figures
out quickly whom she is talking to.

## Skill 14 Analyze Word Choice
### Pages 64–65

1. **(2) judges herself harshly** Option (2) is correct. The
author's choice of the word *idiocy,* with its connotation of
extreme foolishness, shows that Mrs. Dalloway judges herself
harshly. Option (1) is incorrect because *idiocy* is a harsher
judgment than making excuses. Options (3) and (4) are not
the best choice because if Mrs. Dalloway accepted or were
proud of herself she would not accuse herself of idiocy.
Option (5) is incorrect because Mrs. Dalloway is acutely
aware of how others view her.

2. **(1) weathered** Option (1) is correct. Crumpled leather is
creased and rough, and weathered skin is also creased or
wrinkled and rough. Options (2), (3), (4), and (5) are not the
best choices because crumpled leather does not look like a
face that is fat, beautiful, pale, or friendly.

3. **(3) irritated** Option (3) is correct. The words *irritated* and
*annoyed* have similar connotations, so *irritated* is a good
choice to replace *annoyed.* The change would not change the
meaning of the sentence significantly. Options (1), (2), and
(4) are incorrect because *enraged, angry,* and *furious* all have

connotations that are far stronger than *annoyed.* Option (5)
is incorrect because *anxious* means nervous or worried, and
*annoyed* carries the connotation of irritation.

4. **(4) The author emphasizes that Mrs. Dalloway
feels she has little identity or existence.** Option
(4) is correct. The repetition of words with the negative
prefixes *in-* and *un-* emphasizes the negative qualities of
Mrs. Dalloway's existence. Repeating these words has the
effect of stating that Mrs. Dalloway is "not, not, not." Option (1)
is not the best choice because *invisible, unseen,* and *unknown*
are not difficult words that need explanation. Option (2) is
incorrect because nothing in the passage suggests that Mrs.
Dalloway's interior thoughts are deranged. Option (3) is not
the best choice because although her thoughts include what
she believes others think of her, this line indicates this is how
Mrs. Dalloway feels about herself. Option (5) is incorrect
because there is nothing suspicious or threatening in Mrs.
Dalloway's behavior.

5. **(2) Lily enjoys complaining about her life.** Option
(2) is correct. The word *luxury* has a connotation of pleasure;
Lily takes some pleasure in having small things to complain
about. Option (1) is incorrect because the phrase "a luxury of
discontent" suggests her taking some pleasure in the cramped
quarters rather than being truly physically uncomfortable.
Option (3) is not the best answer because Lily is perfectly
happy for the moment in the shabby place, and option (4) is
incorrect because Lily clearly does like Selden. Option (5) is
not the best choice because Lily has no idea what it is like to
be poor, as the last sentence suggests.

6. **(5) small** Option (5) is correct. The word *slip* has several
denotations, or meanings. In this context, it means *small.*
Options (1), (2), (3), and (4) are incorrect because *slip* does
not mean *slick, hidden, dark,* or *depressing* in this particular
context.

7. **(3) aroma** Option (3) is correct. Both *scent* and *aroma*
have positive connotations, so *aroma* replaces *scent* without
significantly changing the meaning of the sentence. Options
(1), (2), (4), and (5) are incorrect because they do not have
the positive connotations that *scent* has. *Smell* has neutral or
negative connotations, while *stench, odor,* and *stink* all have
strongly negative connotations.

8. **(4) victim, fate** Option (4) is correct. Both *victim* and
*fate* have connotations of powerlessness. The other
options—evidently, civilization (option 1); civilization,
produced (option 2); links, bracelet (option 3); and bracelet,
seemed (option 5) are incorrect because none of the words in
those pairings suggests powerlessness.

## Skill 15 Draw Conclusions
### Pages 68–69

1. **(1) He is proud and confident.** Option (1) is the best
choice, based on what Caesar says in lines 46–47: "I rather
tell thee what is to be feared/Than what I fear; for always I
am Caesar." Option (2) is not correct because in lines 48–49
Caesar himself points out his deafness to Antony, rather
than try to hide it. Option (3) is not correct because Caesar's
words are not those of a timid ruler; as he says in lines 46–47,
he is not someone who fears. Option (4) is not the best
choice because though Caesar is suspicious, he bases his

suspicions on observations of one man; he is not suspicious of everyone. Option (5) is not correct; Caesar's comments seem to indicate that he is a close observer of character and judges accordingly.

2. **(2) Caesar is suspicious of Cassius.** Option (2) is the best answer; Caesar reveals his suspicion by saying that Cassius "has a lean and hungry look" and "thinks too much." He concludes that "such men are dangerous." Option (1) is not correct; though Caesar refers to the "lean and hungry look" that Cassius has, he is not commenting on his physical attractiveness. Option (3) is not correct; the text does not indicate that Cassius is bald. Option (4) is not correct; when Caesar says he prefers men who sleep well at night, he is not contrasting them with those who have insomnia but with men who are awake, plotting against him. Option (5) represents a misreading of Caesar's comment that Cassius "thinks too much."

3. **(3) He is fond of plays and music.** Option (3) is correct, based on lines 33–35: "He loves no plays,/As thou dost Antony; he hears no music." Option (1) has no basis in the passage. Option (2) is not a logical conclusion. Though Antony reassures Caesar in lines 23–25, it is apparent that the men trust each other, and reassuring a friend or acquaintance is natural. Option (4) is not correct; no details in the passage give information about Antony's physical appearance. Option (5) is not correct; Caesar earnestly asks Antony for his opinion in lines 50–51. This sort of request is not one that a person makes of a slight acquaintance.

4. **(4) The narrator has fallen in love.** Option (4) is correct. The narrator's description of how he felt while dancing with Charlotte clearly leads to the conclusion that he is in love with her. Option (1) has no basis in the passage; the narrator expresses strong feelings without indicating how long he has known Charlotte. Option (2) is not correct; "I lost sight of every other object" (lines 4–5) does not mean the narrator was blind. Option (3) may or may not be true; though the narrator enjoyed the dance, there is no indication as to whether he is a good dancer. Option (5) is not a logical conclusion; the passage does not indicate for how long they have been dancing or how frequently.

5. **(1) She enjoys dancing.** Option (1) is a logical conclusion based on the statement in lines 23–25 that Charlotte's eyes were "beaming with the sweetest feeling of pure and genuine enjoyment." Option (2) contradicts Charlotte's statement that she is engaged to Albert. Option (3) is not correct because there is no evidence to indicate that the woman is her mother. Option (4) is not correct; Charlotte speaks truly and bluntly about Albert. Option (5) is not correct; though Charlotte is apparently enjoying the dance, we do not know her thoughts and cannot say whether she loves the narrator or not.

## Skill 16 Interpret Overall Style and Structure Pages 72–73

1. **(2) informal** Option (2) is correct because the passage has a conversational tone (including such colloquial phrases as "I tell you" in line 1 and "rolling in it" in lines 6 and line 20–21) and includes sentence fragments (such as "His daughter?" in line 20). Option (1) is incorrect because the passage is not written in standard English and is therefore not formal in

style. Option (3) is incorrect because academic style is not conversational and would not include sentence fragments. Option (4) is not the best answer because although the narrator is serious about what she is saying, her rambling sentences show that she is a silly woman not to be taken seriously. Option (5) is incorrect because the author has not used the complex words and sentences that characterize complex style.

2. **(1) greedy** Option (1) is correct because lines 2–11 and 17–20, among others, make clear that the speaker thinks her brother should give her some of his money and that she hopes he will leave her his money when he dies. Options (2), (3), (4), and (5) are incorrect. Nothing in the passage indicates that the speaker is kind; in fact, her words make clear that she cares only about herself. She certainly is not shy, as the entire passage consists of her stating her opinions. She is angry rather than amused, and she is greedy rather than generous.

3. **(4) the narrator dominates the conversation** Option (4) is correct because the narrator's words are a barrage, uninterrupted by the person to whom she is speaking. The speaker does not pause to ask Bernie's opinion or to give him an opportunity to respond. In fact, she repeatedly dismisses his questions and objections, as in line 16 ("No, that's not the point.") and lines 20–21 ("His daughter? O, she's rolling in it. . . .") Option (1) is incorrect; nothing in the passage indicates that Bernie is not present. Option (2) is incorrect because including only the narrator's words shows that she is inconsiderate and self-centered. Option (3) is incorrect because it is clear from the narrator's words—in line 16, for example—that Bernie does not agree with everything she says. Option (5) is not the best answer because while Bernie may not, in fact, trust the narrator, the author's choice to include only the narrator's words does not indicate whether Bernie does or does not.

4. **(1) time order** Option (1) is correct because the author presents the narrator's words as she says them, in order from beginning to end. Options (2), (3), (4), and (5) are incorrect. The passage does not present a cause and its effect, it does not compare and contrast people or things, it does not present one main idea and details that support it, and it does not present a question and the answer to a question.

5. **(5) detailed descriptions of actions** Option (5) is correct because the passage consists of an action-by-action description of events that occur within a short period of time. Option (1) is incorrect because the style of the passage is not characterized by long, complex sentences; in fact, the passage includes many short, simple sentences and sentence fragments. Option (2) is not the best answer because the passage includes both description and narration. Option (3) is not correct because although the passage is primarily written in standard English, it is not formal. Option (4) is not the best answer because the passage includes both narration and dialogue.

6. **(1) "Where you live? North Side, South Side, or West Side?"** Option (1) is correct because the speaker leaves the word *do* out of the question "Where do you live?" making this nonstandard English. Options (2), (3), (4), and (5) are incorrect because all are examples of standard

English. The words used are standard English words, and the sentences are complete and correct.

**7. (2) informal style** Option (2) is correct because the slang words *ain't and Doll* are nonstandard English and make this sentence an example of informal style. Option (1) is incorrect; conventional style would not include such slang as *ain't* and *Doll*. Option (3) is not the best answer; although readers may find the slang amusing, the speaker is serious about what she is saying. The author has chosen these particular words to portray how the character would speak accurately, not to amuse readers. Option (4) is incorrect because *ain't* is not standard English. Option (5) is incorrect because the sentence is not complex; it is a question expressed in simple, easy-to-understand terms.

**8. (5) time order** Option (5) is correct because, as is often the case in fiction, the author tells events in the diner as they happen, from beginning to end. Options (1), (2), (3), and (4) are incorrect. The passage does not present a question and its answer, one main idea and details that support it, a cause and its effect, or a persuasive argument. These methods of organization would be seen more commonly in nonfiction than in fiction passages such as this one.

## Skill 17 Interpret Tone of a Piece
### Pages 76–77

**1. (3) humorous** Option (3) is correct. Most of the passage consists of a humorous speech based on the idea of someone misinterpreting the law against abandoning sheep without notice. The author includes many examples of humor, including having the sheepherder address the sheep as "my fellow ewes, lambs, and bucks" and appointing a ewe to be the sheep's new leader. Option (1) is not the best answer because although the first two paragraphs of the passage are serious, they merely provide the context the reader needs to appreciate the rest of the article, which is humorous. Options (2) and (4) are incorrect because no words or descriptions in the paragraph indicate that the author is writing with a frustrated or serious, demanding tone. Option (5) is not the best answer because, although the sheepherder's speech shows concern for the sheep, concern is not the overall tone of the piece. The concern expressed in the sheepherder's speech is an element of the passage's humor.

**2. (3) "It could be interpreted to mean that the herder must notify his sheep before leaving them, to prevent emotional trauma, possibly, social breakdown, or obscure ovine behavioral disorders."** Option (3) is correct. This sentence includes a string of silly ideas and intentionally formal words that make clear to readers the author's intention to create a humorous tone. Options (1), (4), and (5) are incorrect because they, by themselves, do not reflect the overall humorous tone of the passage. Option (2) is not the best answer. Although there is a hint of humor in the phrase *nonsheep people*, this sentence alone does not clearly show that the overall tone of the passage will be humorous.

**3. (4) scornful** Option (4) is correct. The author shows his scorn for Babbitt throughout the passage, describing his self-important posturing (as in lines 8–17) and his habit of making vows that he does not keep (lines 27–30 and 31–45).

Option (1) is incorrect because the tone of the passage is not sincerely respectful. Options (2), (3), and (5) are incorrect because there are no words or descriptions in the passage that convey a tone of outrage, sorrow, or tragedy.

**4. (5) "It took but little more time to start his car and edge it into the traffic than it would have taken to walk the three and a half blocks to the club."** Option (5) is correct. This sentence is one of several in the passage that highlight the gap between what Babbitt says and what he actually does. The tone is scornful, as is the overall tone of the excerpt. Option (1) is not the best answer. Even though it does convey a certain crudeness about Babbit, the sentence falls short of clearly establishing a tone. Options (2), (3), and (4) are incorrect because they are emotionally neutral sentences that convey little or no information about the author's attitude toward Babbitt.

**5. (5) scatterbrained** Option (5) is correct. A dash is often used to show abrupt changes in an author's or character's line of thought or speech, and that is exactly how the author uses dashes in this passage. The dashes emphasize that Babbitt's thought process is jumbled and halting, especially in line 17. Options (1), (2), (3), and (4) are incorrect because these dashes do not indicate loudness, profanity, humor, or thoughtfulness.

## Skill 18 Determine Theme
### Pages 80–81

**1. (4) sees his life in a new way** Option (3) is correct. Lines 4–7 are a general statement about "changes in a man's beliefs and scale of values." Option (1) is incorrect because lines 15–16 say that "The mistakes of his life seemed unimportant." This implies that the Bishop had no regrets. Option (2) is also incorrect. In fact, in line 2, the narrator says that the Bishop thought very little about death. Option (3) is not the best answer. Although the Bishop seems to be alone much of the time, in lines 36–37 he mentions two people who visit and ask questions. The passage is not mostly about the Bishop's being alone. In lines 40–41, the narrator says the people who visited *thought* his mind was failing (option 5) but were wrong.

**2. (3) Dying people think about life in new and different ways than others.** Option (3) is correct. Line 12 describes "an enlightenment that came to" the Bishop, and lines 29–35 describe another way in which the Bishop's life had become more "comprehensible" to him. Although lines 36–44 make clear that the people who visit the Bishop do not understand what he is going through (option 1), this is a detail and not the theme of the passage. The narrator states in lines 10–11 that the changes the Bishop is experiencing are "apart from his religious life" (option 2). The author portrays the Bishop as spending much of his time thinking about the past and also makes clear that such thoughts are not a waste of time (option 4) but rather give the Bishop a deeper understanding of life. Nothing in the passage supports the idea that dying people should stay active (option 5). Besides, the Bishop spends his time thinking about his life, not about death.

3. **(2) "But he had an intellectual curiosity about dying; about the changes that took place in a man's beliefs and scale of values."** Option (2) is correct. This sentence is a strong clue that the passage will explore the theme of how a dying man understands life. Option (1) is not the best answer; it merely states what the Bishop did *not* think about. The memory of winters with cousins when he was a child or his student days in Rome (option 3), the fact that it takes him several seconds to gather his thoughts (option 4), or that they might think his mind was failing (option 5) are all incorrect; they are all details, not expressions of the central theme.

4. **(5) how a mature person should behave** Option (5) is correct. The poem discusses various admirable behaviors, leading up to the conclusion that, if you can do all this, "you'll be a Man, my son!" Option (1) is incorrect and not addressed by the poem. Option (2) is incorrect. The poem is not so much about biological age as it is about personal maturity, and many of the examples used would probably not apply well to children. Option (3) is incorrect; the mention of walking "with kings" is not a reference to making friends with them. Option (4) is incorrect. The poem does not suggest disasters can be avoided, but rather gives advice on how to react to them when they do occur.

5. **(4) Acting with maturity and dignity gives you power.** Option (4) is correct. The poem concludes that if you can respond to everything in life with maturity and dignity, "Yours is the Earth and everything that's in it." Option (1) is incorrect. Though the poem mentions betting "all your winnings" on "one turn of pitch-and-toss," the focus is on your reaction to losing all you have, not on the bet itself. Option (2) is incorrect. The poem never mentions standing up for yourself against the injustices of the world; rather, it discusses only how to bear those injustices with quiet dignity. Option (3) is incorrect. The poem focuses on patience, inner strength, and force of will more than physical stamina. Option (5) is incorrect. Though the poem concludes with the words *Man* and *son,* this does not mean that women should not behave this way as well.

6. **(3) "Or, being hated, don't give way to hating,"** Option (3) is correct. This line best supports the idea of responding to adversity with patience and inner strength. Option (1) is incorrect. It is not meeting with both good and bad events, but rather how you respond to those events that the poem discusses. Options (2) and (4) only talk about bad things happening but do not cover how you should respond to them. Option (5) is incorrect. The focus of the poem is not on taking risks, but rather how you should act if those risks turn out badly.

## Skill 19 Compare and Contrast
## Pages 84–85

1. **(3) Bertie thinks quickly.** Option (3) is correct; it names a quality that applies only to Bertie, not to Maurice. Option (1) is not correct because only Maurice is a military man, as implied by his "going out to France for the second time." Option (2) is not correct because Bertie is a Scotchman. Option (4) is incorrect because Bertie's emotions are

described as "not so fine." Option (5) is incorrect because Bertie is described as sentimental.

2. **(5) a fondness for Isabel** Option (5) correctly names what the two men have in common. Option (1) is not correct because Bertie is Scotch and Maurice is English. Option (2) is not correct; they are from different cultural backgrounds, so it is unlikely that they share ancestors. Option (3) is not correct because the passage describes Maurice as a "big fellow with heavy limbs," but there is no mention of Bertie's physical appearance. Option (4) is not correct because Bertie is a barrister and Maurice is a soldier.

3. **(3) He is more emotional than intellectual.** Option (3) is the best answer because in lines 9–10 the narrator describes him as "perhaps oversensitive" and in lines 14–15 as "very sensitive to his own mental slowness." Option (1) is not correct because it contradicts the "mental slowness" the narrator mentions in line 15. Option (2) contradicts the statement that Maurice had "a forehead that flushed painfully." This implies that his feelings are easy to read. Option (4) is not in keeping with the fact that it was Isabel's decision to discontinue her friendship with Bertie. Option (5) is not correct because the narrator reveals that Maurice does not get along with Bertie.

4. **(2) He does not wish to offend Isabel, yet he hints that the relationship must end only "if these were indeed her wishes."** Option (2) is the best choice; Bertie is clever and is looking for a way not to close the door. He thinks Isabel may change her mind with Maurice gone. Option (1) has no basis in the passage—there is no evidence to indicate that Bertie was only pretending to be Isabel's friend. Option (3) is not supported by the passage. The narrator reveals that the men did not like each other, but Bertie did like Isabel. Option (4) is not correct because Bertie is not described as sensitive, nor is there mention of him wanting to avoid conflict. Option (5) is not correct; Bertie was not slow-witted.

5. **(3) a loved one and a summer day** Option (3) is correct. The first line makes clear that the poet is comparing "thee" to a summer day. Option (1) is not supported by the poem, which says nothing about the past. Option (2) is not the best choice; the focus of the comparison is on the loved one. Option (4) is not correct; the suggestions of shadow are made to show only that weather changes, but the loved one's beauty will not. Option (5) is incorrect; there is no mention of autumn.

6. **(4) "You are prettier than a summer day."** Option (4) is correct. The word *more* in line 2 makes the contrast clear. Option (1) is not correct; *temperate* means mild, not hot-tempered. Option (2) is not the best choice; the poem is contrasting the loved one and a summer day, not saying how they are similar. Option (3) is incorrect because it is weather that is unpredictable; nothing is said about the person. Option (5) is not correct; the nature of the person is praised, not criticized, in the poem's opening lines.

7. **(2) summer is not so always so pleasant** Option (2) is correct. The writer has praised the person, saying the person is better than summer, and this option and lines 2–8 explain why. Option (1) is incorrect because there is no suggestion of changing emotions in the poem. Option (3) is incorrect

because there is nothing but praise expressed, not trouble; the lines are literal here, not metaphoric. Option (4) is not the best choice because summer's winds are said to be shaking the buds that grew in May, not that it is May; summer has already arrived. Option (5) is incorrect because nothing in these lines suggests the endurance of beauty.

8. **(5) Summer beauty fades, but his love's beauty will live forever.** Option (5) is correct. The poet describes how summer will come and go, but his love's "eternal summer shall not fade." Options (1) and (2) show similarities; they are comparisons, not contrasts. Options (3) and (4) are not supported in the text.

9. **(4) Your beauty will outlast every summer.** Option (4) is correct. The poem claims that the person's beauty will last forever, despite time and death (and explains how in lines 19–23). Option (1) is incorrect; immortality is impossible, except through the poet's art. Option (2) is incorrect because the poet never includes himself in the discussion. Option (3) is incorrect because no such claim is made explicitly in the poem. Option (5) is incorrect because summer's return every year is not discussed in the poem.

10. **(2) the brief beauty of life to the ongoing life of poetry** Option (2) correctly explains how beauty can go on forever: as long as people read the poem, the beauty of the person continues to exist. It is the poem that continues, not the person. Option (1) is not the best choice because the poem does not say love dies and friendship endures. Option (3) is not correct because the contrast is not between love and changing weather, but between the brief existence of beauty and the long existence of art. Option (4) is not correct because there is no reference of any kind to autumn. Option (5) is not correct because the poem does not refer to its own length, except to say that it will last a long time.

## KEY  Skill 20  Integrate Outside Information Pages 88–89

1. **(5) not enough information** Option (5) is correct. The poem describes how Ozymandias ruled, not how his rule ended. Although any of options—he was defeated (option 1); he grew old and died (option 2), he fell victim to disease (option 3), or he was assassinated (option 4)—could have happened, there is no information to confirm or deny any of them.

2. **(3) the ruler's military skill or power** Option (3) is correct. The reasoning was that if the ruler were not a god or did not have the approval of a divinity, he could not have risen to rule or be successful in battle. Thus, if a ruler had military skill and power, he was seen as divine. Option (1) is not the best choice because the monuments were built as a result of the king being considered divine, not the other way around. Option (2) is not the best choice because the stories were told after the rulers were considered divine. Option (4) is not correct because illiteracy would not have anything to do with the belief in a king's divinity. Option (5) is incorrect; it does not relate to the issue of a king's divinity and it is not true—many ancient religions were quite complex.

3. **(4) the impermanence of human works** Option (4) is correct. Shelley's poem points out that nothing human endures forever. There is no evidence or discussion of a competing kingdom (option 1). Option (2) is not correct because the wealth of the kingdom is gone today, and a shattered fragment would not show the wealth. The superiority or inferiority of ancient cultures (option 3) cannot be assessed from the poem. Option (5) is not the best choice because the poem clearly shows the limits of time, though the art may hold appeal as a historical artifact.

4. **(4) their records and artifacts have disappeared** Option (4) is correct. Like Ozymandias, the information is simply gone, and there are no existing records to study or verify. How powerful ancient societies were (option 1) or weren't cannot be determined without the records. Option (2) is incorrect because we do not know enough about ancient societies' beliefs and customs to make a judgment. Option (3) is not the best option because there is no information to confirm or deny the possibility that the cities were destroyed by fire. Option (5) is incorrect because ancient cultures are indeed worth detailed study, and studies are conducted when information is available.

5. **(2) improving India in a way that is acceptable to the British** Option (2) best summarizes Purun Dass's efforts; he remains Indian but accepts and furthers British projects. Option (1) is incorrect; there is no evidence in the passage that Dass does anything toward independence. Option (3) is incorrect; nothing in the passage shows Dass trying to preserve his heritage. Purun Dass doesn't block the British effort (option 4) but helps it. He doesn't make the Maharajah look bad (option 5); instead, he always makes sure the Maharajah gets the credit.

6. **(3) Purun Dass's attempt to balance his role between the British and the Indians** Option (3) is correct. Purun Dass is aware of his delicate position. He must steer a middle course between his countrymen, the Maharajah, and the ruling English. He avoids clashes of culture when he can. There is no evidence in the passage that Purun Dass resents the British (option 1). Option (2) is not the best choice because Purun Dass is sensitive to the Maharajah and is trying to improve the country while staying within British expectations. Option (4) is incorrect because there is no relationship between Purun Dass's political position and British rule; Purun Dass is responsible for his rise through his own ability to work the system. That he is unable to makes changes in Indian life (option 5) is contradicted by the passage.

7. **(3) Indian culture and customs would have come to prevail in the country.** Option (3) is correct. With Indians assuming complete control of their government, it makes sense that their culture would become the prevailing one, as indeed it has. Option (1) is not correct because independence brings much change—that is the point of changing to self-rule. Option (2) is not correct because traces of English culture would have permeated Indian culture and values, as shown in the example of Purun Dass, and survived in post-British India, as indeed they have. Option (4) is incorrect because independence means that Britain gave up its power over India in all ways. It does not follow logically that the two countries would become enemies (option 5) as soon as the tension of the struggle for independence ended.

# Pretest Answer Sheet: Language Arts, Reading

Name: _____ Class: _____ Date: _____

| | | | | |
|---|---|---|---|---|
| 1 ①②③④⑤ | 5 ①②③④⑤ | 9 ①②③④⑤ | 13 ①②③④⑤ | 17 ①②③④⑤ |
| 2 ①②③④⑤ | 6 ①②③④⑤ | 10 ①②③④⑤ | 14 ①②③④⑤ | 18 ①②③④⑤ |
| 3 ①②③④⑤ | 7 ①②③④⑤ | 11 ①②③④⑤ | 15 ①②③④⑤ | 19 ①②③④⑤ |
| 4 ①②③④⑤ | 8 ①②③④⑤ | 12 ①②③④⑤ | 16 ①②③④⑤ | 20 ①②③④⑤ |

# Official GED Practice Test Form PA Answer Sheet: Language Arts, Reading

Name: _____ Class: _____ Date: _____

Time Started: _____

Time Finished: _____

| | | | | |
|---|---|---|---|---|
| 1 ①②③④⑤ | 5 ①②③④⑤ | 9 ①②③④⑤ | 13 ①②③④⑤ | 17 ①②③④⑤ |
| 2 ①②③④⑤ | 6 ①②③④⑤ | 10 ①②③④⑤ | 14 ①②③④⑤ | 18 ①②③④⑤ |
| 3 ①②③④⑤ | 7 ①②③④⑤ | 11 ①②③④⑤ | 15 ①②③④⑤ | 19 ①②③④⑤ |
| 4 ①②③④⑤ | 8 ①②③④⑤ | 12 ①②③④⑤ | 16 ①②③④⑤ | 20 ①②③④⑤ |

# [ Acknowledgements ]

For permission to reproduce copyrighted material, grateful acknowledgment is made to the following sources:

From THE INVISIBLE PYRAMID by Loren Eiseley. Copyright © 1970 by Loren Eiseley. Reproduced by permission of Scribner, an imprint of Simon & Schuster Adult Publishing Group. **(p. 13)**

"Let America be America Again" from THE COLLECTED POEMS OF LANGSTON HUGHES by Langston Hughes. Copyright © 1994 by The Estate of Langston Hughes. Reproduced by permission of Alfred A. Knopf, a division of Random House, Inc. **(p. 19)**

From THE REMAINS OF THE DAY by Kazuo Ishiguro. Copyright © 1989 by Kazuo Ishiguro. Reproduced by permission of Alfred A. Knopf, a division of Random House, Inc. **(p. 23)**

From FUNERAL GAMES by Mary Renault. Copyright © 1981 by Mary Renault. Reproduced by permission of Curtis Brown, Ltd. London, on behalf of The Estate of Mary Renault. **(p. 27)**

From SPOON RIVER ANTHOLOGY by Edgar Lee Masters. Copyright © 1962 by The Estate of Edgar Lee Masters. Reproduced by permission of Hilary Masters. **(p. 35)**

From CROSSING TO SAFETY by Wallace Stegner. Copyright © 1987 by Wallace Stegner. Reproduced by permission of Random House, Inc. **(p. 37)**

From THE JUNGLE by Upton Sinclair. Copyright 1905, 1906 by Upton Sinclair. Reproduced by permission of Viking Penguin, a division of Penguin Group (USA). **(p. 38)**

From HOOP DREAMS by Ben Joravsky. Copyright © 1995 Ben Joravsky. Reproduced by permission of Ben Joravsky and Kartemquin Educational Films. **(p. 40)**

From "Nothing to Sneeze At" from NATIONAL GEOGRAPHIC, October 2001. Copyright © 2001 by National Geographic Society. Reproduced by permission of National Geographic Society. **(p. 41)**

From ANNE OF GREEN GABLES by L.M. Montgomery. Copyright © by the Heirs of L.M. Montgomery. Reproduced by permission of the Heirs of L.M. Montgomery. **(p. 45)**

"May Day" from THE COLLECTED POEMS OF SARA TEASDALE by Sara Teasdale. (New York: Macmillan, 1937). Reproduced by permission of Scribner, an imprint of Simon & Schuster Adult Publishing Group. **(p. 46)**

"Father and Son" from THE WAY IT IS: NEW & SELECTED POEMS by William Stafford. Copyright © 1973, 1988 by The Estate of William Stafford. Reproduced by permission of Graywolf Press, Saint Paul, Minnesota. **(p. 47)**

"The Old Men Admiring Themselves in the Water" by William Butler Yeats from THE COLLECTED WORKS OF W. B. YEATS, VOLUME I: THE POEMS, REVISED, edited by Richard J. Finneran. Copyright 1928 by The Macmillan Company and renewed © 1956 by Georgie Yeats. Reproduced by permission of Scribner, an imprint of Simon & Schuster Adult Publishing Group. **(p. 50)**

From THE METAMORPHOSIS by Franz Kafka, translated by Stanley Corngold. Translation copyright © 1972 by Stanley Corngold. Reproduced by permission of Bantam Books, Inc., a division of Random House, Inc. **(p. 59)**

From SLEEPING AT THE STARLIGHT MOTEL by Bailey White. Copyright © 1995 by Bailey White. Reproduced by permission of Da Capo Press, a member of Perseus Books Group. **(p. 62)**

From MRS.DALLOWAY by Virginia Woolf, Copyright 1925 by Houghton Mifflin Harcourt Publishing Company and copyright renewed © 1953 by Leonard Woolf. Reproduced by permission of Houghton Mifflin Harcourt Publishing Company. **(p. 64)**

From FRIDA: A BIOGRAPHY OF FRIDA KAHLO by Hayden Herrera. Copyright © 1983 by Hayden Herrera. Reproduced by permission of HarperCollins Publishers, Inc. **(p. 70)**

"Spring is like a perhaps hand" from COMPLETE POEMS: 1904-1962 by E. E. Cummings, edited by George J. Firmage. Copyright 1923, 1925, 1951, 1953, © 1991 by the Trustees for the E. E. Cummings Trust. Copyright © 1976 by George James Firmage. Reproduced by permission of Liveright Publishing Corporation. **(p. 71)**

From THE LONELY PASSION OF JUDITH HEARNE by Brian Moore. Copyright © 1955, 1983 by Brian Moore. Reproduced by permission of Little, Brown and Company, Inc. **(p. 72)**

From "The Derelict" by Mark Allen Boone. Copyright © by Mark Allen Boone. Reproduced by permission of Mark Allen Boone. **(p. 73)**

"When You are Old" by William Butler Yeats from THE COLLECTED WORKS OF W. B. YEATS, VOLUME I: THE POEMS, REVISED, edited by Richard J. Finneran. Copyright 1928 by The Macmillan Company; copyright renewed © 1956 by Georgie Yeats. Reproduced by permission of Scribner, an imprint of Simon & Schuster Adult Publishing Group. **(p. 74)**

From CACTUS TRACKS & COWBOY PHILOSOPHY by Baxter Black. Copyright © 1997 by Baxter Black. Reproduced by permission of Crown Publishers, a division of Random House, Inc. **(p. 76)**

From DEATH COMES FOR THE ARCHBISHOP by Willa Cather. Copyright 1927, 1929 by Willa Cather and renewed 1955, © 1957 by The Executors of the Estate of Willa Cather. Reproduced by permission of Alfred A. Knopf, a division of Random House, Inc. **(p. 80)**

"The Blind Man" from COMPLETE SHORT STORIES OF D.H. LAWRENCE by D.H. Lawrence. Copyright 1922 by Thomas Seltzer, Inc. and renewed copyright 1950 by Frieda Lawrence. Reproduced by permission of Viking Penguin, a division of Penguin Group (USA) Inc. **(p. 84)**

From FRAGMENTS OF THE ARK by Louise Meriwether, published by Simon & Schuster. Copyright © 1994 by Louise Meriwether. Reproduced by permission of Ellen Levine Agency, Inc. on behalf of the author. **(p. 4)**